CW01190787

A Tale of Two Towns

A HISTORY OF MEDIEVAL GLASGOW

EDITED BY NEIL BAXTER

First published 2007 by
Neil Baxter Associates, Glasgow
on behalf of Glasgow City Council

Text: the contributors
Design: Jon Jardine (mail@jonjardine.com)

Copyright © the contributors / Neil Baxter / Glasgow City Council 2007
All rights reserved.

ISBN: 978-0-9537149-3-3

A catalogue record for this book is available from the British Library.

Image overleaf: document of 1558 with seals of the archdiocese and the burgh of Glasgow

Acknowledgements

THIS BOOK IS ONE OF a number of initiatives promoted by Glasgow's Local History and Archaeology Working Group. All of the members of that Group have contributed their time and enthusiasm to help with its funding and production. However the Chair of the Group, Bailie Catherine McMaster deserves particular thanks for her drive and commitment. She has also provided constructive criticism of the original proposal and the content as this has evolved. Kate Dargie, Local Heritage Officer and her senior colleagues Alistair MacDonald and Cathy Johnston have also helped to ensure that this publication meets the aspirations of the Working Group.

A number of other individuals have helped with fact checking and with the illustrations. Among these Irene O'Brien, Susan Pacitti and Dario Marchetti merit particular thanks for their assistance with providing images and copyright permissions. Ellen McAdam's advice on the content and narrative style of the book has been immensely helpful. Others who have assisted with information are the Rev. Tom Davidson Kelly and Ian MacNair. Invaluable final proof checking was undertaken by Vivienne Nicoll and Alison Shaw.

Of course those who have contributed most to this publication are the authors themselves. They have all gone well beyond their original remit of providing entertaining and informative essays on their respective specialist subjects. James Macaulay has supplied a number of prints, among them the coloured first edition of the Slezer view which serves, at James' prompting, as the cover of the book and to illustrate the title pages of each essay. Norman Shead, David Sellar and Mary McHugh have provided meticulous additional research and have provided significant guidance through the minefield of conflicting dates and details.

David Sellar has asked that his personal thanks be conveyed to his colleague Norman Shead for the latter's guidance on the detailed content of David's chapter on Law, Courts and People. Michael Lynch, Patricia Dennison and Donny O'Rourke have worked towards ensuring that the book goes well beyond historical analysis to give a real insight to the everyday lives of medieval Glaswegians. Working with this group of brilliant historians and commentators has been consistently entertaining and immensely rewarding.

My final thank you is reserved for my colleagues Theresa White and Jon Jardine. Theresa has exercised her usual patience and skill as the book has gone through its numerous typescripts and has demonstrated her habitual tolerance over successive revisions, amendments and endless editorial tweaks. Jon Jardine has, as ever, provided a design which enhances the authors' wisdom and will give readers much additional delight. His skill in matching images to narrative, his patient redrawing of maps and plans and his inspired colourising of black and white images contribute immensely to the quality and readability of this publication. And to Josh McGuire, once again, simply thanks!

Neil Baxter, June 2007

Funders

The Local History and Archaeology Working Group is grateful to the following organisations whose funding has made this publication possible:

Glasgow Cathedral, Glasgow City Council, Scottish Enterprise Glasgow, The Archdiocese of Glasgow, The Church of Scotland, Presbytery of Glasgow, The Dean of Guild Court Trust, The Merchants House of Glasgow, The Society of Friends of Glasgow Cathedral, The Trades House of Glasgow, The United Diocese of Glasgow and Galloway in the Scottish Episcopal Church, Unite

Photography and illustrations

We are grateful to the following people and organisations for the use of the photographs and images in this book:

Aberdeen Art Gallery and Museum Museums Collections, Colin Beattie, Chris Brown, Alan Crumlish, Archdiocese of Glasgow, Culture & Sport Glasgow, Dr E Patricia Dennison, Glasgow City Council (Culture and Sport Glasgow, Museums), Archives and Special Collections, The Mitchell Library (Culture and Sport Glasgow), Glasgow Building Preservation Trust, Glasgow City Council Development & Regeneration Services, Headland Archaeology, Historic Scotland, Jon Jardine, Royal Museum of Fine Arts, Antwerp © Reproductiefonds, Prof Michael Lynch, Dr James Macaulay, Dario Marchetti, Marsh's Library, Dublin, David Simon, SUAT Ltd , Trustees of the National Library of Scotland, Mike R Vosper Coins (www.vosper4coins.co.uk)

Every effort has been made to obtain copyright clearance on all the images within this publication – please address any enquiries to mail@neilbaxterassoc.co.uk

Contents

The authors	1
A message from the Lord Provost	3
A message from Bailie McMaster	4
Foreword	5
Timeline	6
Introduction PROFESSOR MICHAEL LYNCH	8
Greater Glasgow NORMAN F SHEAD	20
Law, Courts and People DAVID SELLAR	30
The Role of the Church DR MARY MCHUGH	38
A Tale of Two Towns DR E PATRICIA DENNISON	46
The Great Buildings of Early Glasgow DR JAMES MACAULAY	56
Daily Life, Disease and Death DR E PATRICIA DENNISON	68
The Glasgow Tales DONNY O'ROURKE	76
Bibliography	87
Glossary	89
Index	91

In omni diversitate fortune Infelicissimum est genus Infortunii
qui potuit tranquillam ducere vitam,
et letos stabili claudere fine dies   s. stabili

Ee tamen Infelix scelerisque penitet acti
quis sine facinus plangere sepe solet

Disce silium ferre pacienter ut psalmus canit

liber domini Thome Knox notarii publici

tempore benedic deum et
pete ab eo ut vias tuas dirigat

The authors

Neil Baxter (Editor)
Principal of Neil Baxter Associates, an architectural, urban and interpretation consultancy, Neil is Development Director of Glasgow Building Preservation Trust, a Director of the Prince of Wales' North Highland Initiative, a former part-time lecturer in architectural history in the Mackintosh School of Architecture and former guest tutor in urban studies at Glasgow University. In addition to co-authorship of the life of Pat Lally, *Lazarus Only Done it Once* (London, 2000) he is editor of *Fragments: A Life in Cities*, the autobiography of David Mackay of MBM Arquitectes (Barcelona, 2005) and author of *The Wee Green Book: A History of Glasgow Green* (Glasgow, 2007).

Dr E Patricia Dennison
Pat Dennison is Director of the Centre for Scottish Urban History in the School of History at Edinburgh University. Her extensive consultancy experience is in the documentary assessment of archaeological sites, both before and after excavation. She was the historical consultant to the archaeological research at the Scottish Parliament site. In addition to her co-authorship of over twenty Burgh Survey volumes she is co-editor of *A New History of Aberdeen* (East Linton, 2002) and author of *Holyrood and Canongate: A Thousand Years of History* (Edinburgh, 2005)

Prof Michael Lynch
Formerly Professor of Scottish History at the University of Edinburgh, Michael Lynch is among Scotland's most renowned and respected urban historians. A trustee of the National Museums of Scotland he is a former Chair of the Ancient Monuments Board for Scotland and a past President of the Society of Antiquaries of Scotland. His extensive list of published works includes: *Scotland A New History* (London, 1990), he is general editor of the *Oxford Companion to Scottish History* (Oxford, 2001) and co-editor of *A New History of Aberdeen* (East Linton, 2002).

Dr James Macaulay
Former Senior Lecturer in Architectural History at the Mackintosh School of Architecture, James is an Honorary Research Fellow at the University of Glasgow. He is a former Chairman of the Society of Architectural Historians of Great Britain and current Chairman of the Society of Friends of Glasgow Cathedral. His published work includes *The Gothic Revival 1745-1845* (Glasgow, 1975), *The Classical Country House in Scotland* (London, 1987) and *Glasgow School of Art: Charles Rennie Mackintosh* (London, 1993).

Dr Mary McHugh
Archivist to the Archdiocese of Glasgow, Mary is a lecturer in Scottish history and church history at the Scotus College, Bearsden and Secretary of the Scottish Catholic Heritage Commission. She is currently undertaking research on Scottish Catholicism in the nineteenth and twentieth centuries. Her published works include a number of church histories including St Patrick's, Shieldmuir and St Kevin's, Bargeddie and articles, *The Religious Conditions of the Highlands and Islands* in the Innes Review (1984) and the chapter on education in T M Devine (ed.) *St Mary's, Hamilton: A Social History 1846-1996* (Edinburgh, 1995).

Donny O'Rourke
One of Scotland's best known poets, Donny O'Rourke is also a broadcaster, filmmaker, university teacher, editor, journalist and critic. He is a former Head of Arts and Documentaries at Scottish Television and a former executive producer at BBC Scotland. His published collections include *The Waistband and Other Poems* (Edinburgh, 1997), *On A Roll: A Jena Notebook* (Edinburgh, 2001), *Poetry's Waiting Room* (Nuremberg, 2005), and *One Light Burning* (Glasgow, 2007).

David Sellar
An Honorary Fellow of the School of Law at the University of Edinburgh, David is a well known legal and family historian and expert on Scots law. He is a past Chairman of Council of the Scottish History Society and a former Vice-President of the Society of Antiquaries of Scotland. His published works include co-authorship of *The Scottish Legal Tradition* (Edinburgh, 1991), editorship of *Moray Provinces and People* (Edinburgh, 1993) and the chapter on *Hebridean Sea Kings* in Cowan and MacDonald (eds.) *Alba: Celtic Scotland in the Middle Ages* (East Linton, 2000).

Norman F Shead
Norman F Shead is an Honorary Research Fellow in History at the University of Glasgow. Formerly a principal teacher of history and a Fellow of the Royal Historical Society, he was a member of the editorial team for volumes six and seven of *Scotichronicon* and both a contributor and section editor of the *Atlas of Scottish History to 1707* (Edinburgh, 1996). He is joint editor of the *Heads of Religious Houses in Scotland from the Twelfth to the Sixteenth Centuries* (Edinburgh, 2001).

Uni'ug' no martirs offm. Dile
Sapientia iuat. ep. Gaudes gaude
x. Emulor. Alleluia Sileé e e dcé. O

ultum tuum deprecabu

bis adoliuentur regi uirgines

A message from the Lord Provost

Glasgow's medieval heritage has for too long been overlooked. Apart from the cathedral and Provand's Lordship almost all trace of the hilltop town created by the first Glaswegians has been swept away by subsequent generations. The first merchant centre, on the flat plain between the River Clyde and the Molendinar Burn, is also long gone.

Yet Glasgow's origins are of profound importance towards understanding how this city grew from modest beginnings to become first a place of pilgrimage then a merchant centre and ultimately an industrial powerhouse of world significance.

Previous accounts of pre-Reformation Glasgow have been aimed at an academic audience. This book is the first exploration of Glasgow's medieval origins designed for a general readership. It will inform Glaswegians with an interest in how their city was formed and visitors who want to explore the whole history of this remarkable place.

A Tale of Two Towns is the result of the vision and endeavour of the Local History and Archaeology Working Group, chaired by Bailie Catherine McMaster, and of many others who have given their time and energy to the task of revisiting a city too long lost to the popular imagination. Its rediscovery recognises the contribution of our forebears to the evolution of the great city of Glasgow.

Rt Hon The Lord Provost, Councillor Bob Winter

A message from Bailie McMaster

THIS BOOK WAS COMMISSIONED BY Glasgow's Local History and Archaeology Working Group which includes representation from Glasgow and Strathclyde Universities; the West of Scotland Archaeology Service; The Archdiocese of Glasgow; The Roman Catholic Church in Scotland; The Church of Scotland; The Scottish Episcopal Church, Culture and Sport Glasgow and representatives from Glasgow City Council's Land Services and Development and Regeneration teams.

The publication of this account of Glasgow's early history is the outcome of a process which began with the production of the, hugely popular, Medieval City Map in summer 2006. Since then, what might be described as Glasgow's first ever history, the *Life of St Kentigern*, commissioned by Bishop Jocelin at the end of the twelfth century, has been returned to the city – at least in facsimile. At a special service in Glasgow Cathedral in March 2007, copies of *Kentigern: De Vita Sua* were presented to the cathedral itself, the Archdiocese of Glasgow, the Mitchell Library and to Marsh's Library, Dublin, repository of the most intact original copy of the book, which kindly gave permission for this precious volume to be copied. This is the first time that the original life of the city's patron saint has been lodged in Glasgow for nearly 450 years.

A Tale of Two Towns is the result of eight months of dedicated hard work by its authors, its editor Neil Baxter, the designer, Jon Jardine, and the many others who have given advice and helped with the research and illustrations. The brief for the book was not to provide the definitive history of early Glasgow – that will require much further research and endeavour – but to create the first detailed reappraisal of medieval Glasgow of the new millennium.

This book is aimed at a wide audience and explores a range of topics from the historical and geographical contexts to the daily struggle of the ordinary folk of early Glasgow. *A Tale of Two Towns* also considers the roles of the church, the law and trade in Glasgow's early centuries. An exploration of the evolution of the city's important early buildings and the townscape, as it evolved over Glasgow's first five centuries, is also included. The final chapter of the book visits a group of characters who might well have inhabited the Glasgow of the middle ages.

Through this new publication a Glasgow, almost lost to memory, re-emerges as a vibrant reality. This endeavour is another major step towards revealing the origins of a city which, as one of the authors comments, took root among the ancient kingdoms of Scotland and has since grown, flourished and endured.

Bailie Catherine McMaster,
Chair, Local History and Archaeology Working Group

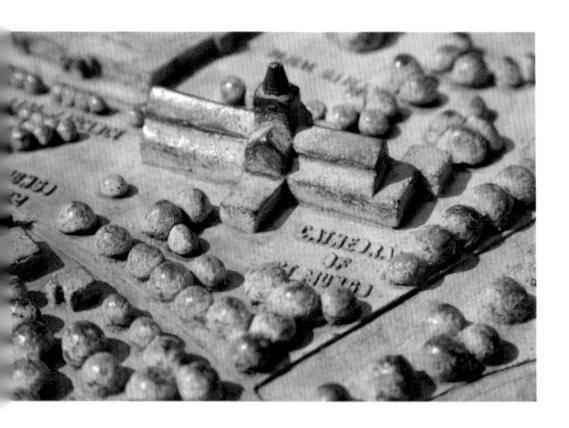

Foreword

Towards the end of 2006, six of Scotland's most respected historians and one of our best-loved poets were set the task of bringing the history of medieval Glasgow to a new audience. Glasgow's origins are obscure. Its early history, like the city's name itself, has been the subject of much conjecture. On the roots of the name, there is still no consensus, other than general agreement that the fanciful notion that it is an arcane ancient dialect rendering of 'The Dear Green Place' is a romantic invention. However, as Michael Lynch implicitly acknowledges in the opening line of his introduction, this epithet still serves well to describe the city.

The written and archaeological evidence of Glasgow's first centuries is both slight and problematic. The historian's task, often one of sifting through a considerable volume of evidence to get at the facts, is much more challenging here, where much has to be gleaned from scraps and passing references.

As original source material is very limited, each of the authors in this volume has drawn from the same body of evidence to explore their separate topics. While, as far as possible, overt repetition has been avoided, several chapters inevitably use the same sources to inform and illuminate their various topics. Where repeated information contributes to the development of a theme or argument it has been spared the editorial red pen. Thus readers are asked to tolerate the repetition of some facts or references.

This book is designed to set the context; geographical, political, ecclesiastical and legal in which early Glasgow evolved. These issues are closely examined by Norman Shead, David Sellar and Mary McHugh. The book also sets out to explore the physical make-up of the town, or towns, of Glasgow's first centuries. The design and construction of Glasgow's first buildings, domestic, utilitarian and grand, is also considered in some detail. Patricia Dennison considers how the townscape evolved while James Macaulay reviews the architecture of the cathedral (in its various incarnations), the friaries and Glasgow's early educational establishments.

The structure of early Glasgow grew and evolved through the influence of the church, of trade, of manufacture and the necessity to house and provide for its, steadily growing, population. The final chapter is deliberately quite different in narrative style from the rest of the book. It, fittingly, focuses upon the fact that it was the people who made Glasgow, just as the people of many nations continue to give this city its unique character. Donny O'Rourke's exploration of the lives of a group of the city's late fifteenth century inhabitants is inspired by one of the greatest chroniclers of the middle ages, Geoffrey Chaucer.

The authors who have contributed to this book are among the most distinguished writers and historians in Scotland. They have provided significant insights into how the city, founded upon the shrine of St Kentigern, grew and developed through the five centuries of the medieval period. Starting out as a place of pilgrimage it evolved into a mercantile and industrial centre, the precursor to Glasgow's remarkable growth into a world city of trade, manufacture and innovation. This is a city built upon a powerful story. Its story is among the most remarkable of any city.

Neil Baxter

Timeline

7th century

614AD — St Kentigern's death

12th century

1109-1114 — Bishop Michael
1114-1118 — Bishop John appointed sometime between these dates
1114-1124 — Inquest of David (later David I) recorded
1124-1153 — reign of King David I
1136 — first cathedral consecrated
1147 — Bishop John buried in Jedburgh
1147-1164 — Bishop Herbert
1153-1165 — reign of King Malcolm IV
1161 — Glasgow's chapter first mentioned in a document
1161 — Pope Alexander III decreed that everyone within the diocese of Glasgow make an annual pilgrimage to the shrine of St Kentigern
1164-1174 — Bishop Ingram
1165-1214 — reign of King William I, the Lion
1173 — Archbishop Thomas Becket of Canterbury canonised
1175 — Glasgow granted 'special daughter' status by the pope
1175-1178 — bishop's burgh charter granted and right to hold a weekly market
1175-1199 — Bishop Jocelin
1189 — cathedral destroyed by fire
1189-1198 — right to hold an annual fair granted
1197 — cathedral re-consecrated
1199 — Bishop Jocelin buried in Melrose

13th century

1200-1202 — Bishop William Malveisin
1208-1232 — Bishop Walter de St Albans
1211 — second papal bull stipulates annual pilgrimage to Glasgow
1222 — Royal Burgh of Dumbarton founded by Alexander II
1225 — Scottish bishops authorised to set up their own council
1233-1258 — Bishop William de Bondington
1233 — work begins on the cathedral which still survives today
1235 — Glasgow troop attacked an Irish force (which had been involved in war in Galloway)
1238 — second archdeaconry created in Glasgow
1241 — a royal charter granted the bishop the rights of 'free forest'
1246 — papal bull granted an indulgence to all the faithful who contributed to the completion of the church which the Dominicans (the Friars Preachers of Glasgow) had begun to build
1247 — Gerard of Rome was canon of Renfrew
1248 — fourteen prebends
1249-1258 — first mention of a Glasgow chancellor
1258 — Bishop Bondington granted the canons the right to elect the dean
1259-1268 — Bishop John de Cheam
1266 — sub-dean to deputise for the dean in office
1271-1316 — Bishop Robert Wishart
1275 — Alexander III ordered the men of Dumbarton not to trouble the men of Glasgow
1286 — first mention of first bridge over the Clyde
1286 — death of Alexander III

14th century

1303 — Robert the Bruce appointed sheriff of Lanark and Ayr
1304 — Bishop Robert Wishart claimed that his officials had an immemorial right to levy tolls on the burgesses of Rutherglen for all goods traded in Glasgow
1305 — trial of Wallace in London
1306-1329 — reign of King Robert I (Robert the Bruce)
1315-1316 — famine
1320 — chapel dedicated to St Thomas built
1325 — sixteen prebends
1328 — Robert I stopped in Glasgow en route to Ulster
1349 — Black Death reached Scotland
1367-1387 — Bishop Walter de Wardlaw (appointed the first Scottish cardinal in 1383)
1387-1408 — Bishop Matthew Glendinning

15th century

1401 — twenty-three prebends
1424 — James I stopped in Glasgow en route to Ayr
1426-1446 — Bishop John Cameron

1427	Bishop John Cameron made chancellor
1429	act passed requiring burgesses to attend musters equipped for war
1430	twenty-nine prebends
1436	act passed setting closing time in pubs
1437-1460	reign of King James II
1440	thirty-two individual canons' dwellings
1444	Glasgow acquired a town clerk
1447	'Vico Fullorum' (the street of the fullers) first mentioned in town's records
1454	'Walcargate' first mentioned in town's records
1450	James II forbade Rutherglen from interfering with the trading privileges of Glasgow
1450	barony of Glasgow raised in standing to a regality by royal charter
1450	Glasgow Green becomes, effectively Britain's first public park
1451	foundation of the university
1454	John Stewart described as the "first provost that was in Glasgow"
1455-1473	Bishop Andrew de Durisdeer
1460	new altar to St Kentigern built in cathedral
1460	first mention of Glasgow Grammar School
1464	founding of St Nicholas Hospital
1470	(and 50 years after) side altars added to cathedral
1471	Provand's Lordship built
1472	bishop of St Andrews made an archbishop
1473	house of the Observant Franciscans founded
1483-1508	Archbishop Robert Blacader
1488	death of James III
1489	James IV stopped in Glasgow en route to besiege Duchal and Dumbarton Castles
late 15th C	thirty-two prebends
1490	bishop authorised to have an official tron, or weigh beam and to charge customs on all who were obliged to weigh their goods there
1491	lepers chapel built
1492	Glasgow becomes an archbishopric
1495	James IV stopped in Glasgow before and after an expedition to the Western Isles
1495	Aberdeen University founded

16th century

1500	new chapel to St Kentigern founded
1501	first reference to a town council
1508-1523	Archbishop Beaton
1518-1532	Franciscan's Church improved
1520s	ashlar curtain wall built around the bishop's castle
1524	Blacader's Hospital founded
1525	Collegiate Church of St Mary of Loreto and St Anne founded
1535	Glasgow accounts for 36 percent of the taxation levied on the Upper Clyde burghs
1544	Earl of Lennox besieged in Glasgow by the Earl of Arran
1545	brawl between St Andrew's and Glasgow clergy in the cathedral
1560	acceptance of the Protestant Reformation by the Scottish Parliament
1560	houses of the friars abandoned
1560	second Archbishop Beaton fled to France taking the cathedral's treasures with him for safe keeping
1561	Mary, Queen of Scots and her Council instructed a property survey as a means of assessing ecclesiastical wealth
1570	St Mary of Loreto and St Anne's Church destroyed
1573	Old Wynd first laid out
1573	return of Protestant Archbishop
1574	Greyfriars, Rottenrow and Drygate Ports permanently locked because of an outbreak of plague
1575	new well dug in Gallowgate
1580s/90s	first maps of Glasgow drawn by Timothy Pont
1588	Trongate shifted
1588	Lindsay's Port first mentioned
1589	significant repairs to Franciscan's Church
1594	Glasgow accounted for 61 percent of the region's taxation
1599	Tron Kirk built

17th century on

1626	Tolbooth built
1630-1636	Tron Kirk steeple substantially altered
1636	Glasgow elevated to the status of royal burgh
1639	rental roll, recording the income of all the Scottish burghs, placed Glasgow third
1651-1685	reign of King Charles II
1652	severe fire engulfed alleys and closes off the Saltmarket and Trongate
1670	Dominican church struck by lightning
1789	the French Revolution resulted in the loss or destruction of the relics of four centuries of Glasgow's history (treasures taken to Paris by the second Archbishop Beaton in 1560)
1870	University moved to Gilmorehill

A note about dates

The dates given on this timeline and in the book itself for bishops, archbishops and kings relate to their reigns, as opposed to being life dates.

life was short, unrelenting and almost indescribably

tough

Introduction

PROFESSOR MICHAEL LYNCH

Origins and evidence

This book attempts to recapture the early history of 'The Dear Green Place' in its many facets. Much of the material on which the book rests is scattered or fragmented and it is often difficult to interpret. Surviving records were not compiled with a view to informing twenty-first century observers.

The language in which early records are written can pose a formidable barrier. References to the organisation and terminology of the medieval church or of the law add to the difficulty. A good deal of the later literature on the distant past of Glasgow and Glaswegians poses its own problems.

The accuracy of most studies of Glasgow written before the twentieth century is questionable although they do contain a wealth of information. More modern studies tend to be academic and specialist. Information about the beliefs and fears of Glasgow's medieval inhabitants is mostly to be found in academic journals. Insights into how people actually lived, worked and died is largely confined to archaeologists' reports.

Much of the past, of course, has disappeared. The evidence lies either below ground, whether excavated or not, or has been lost to memory. What little does remain of medieval Glasgow – such as the cathedral and Provand's Lordship – poses the difficulty of fully understanding what seems all too familiar. Even such an outstanding surviving monument as the cathedral requires a concentrated effort to imagine as it was in its heyday. Even then, the question needs to be asked: which heyday? It is easy to make the mistake of viewing the medieval past as a static period.

Glasgow's mother church was the centre of an enormous, sprawling diocese, a mecca for pilgrims and, very unusually for a cathedral, also a parish church for the town's inhabitants. This huge building was continually in process of building, reconstruction, extension and repair throughout five medieval centuries. The same is true of the burgh itself.

In a sense Glasgow's middle ages are still with us. The story of Kentigern (or Mungo), Glasgow's patron saint, harks back to the sixth century AD. The dedication of the cathedral to St Mungo was deeply enough engrained to survive the Protestant Reformation, although, officially, the cathedral came to be known as the 'High Church'. Yet the process of adopting Kentigern took place some 600 years after his death.

Much of what is known of the city's saint is contained in two *Lifes* of St Kentigern, commissioned by two twelfth century Glasgow bishops, Bishop Herbert (1147-64) and Bishop Jocelin (1175-99). These early leaders of the Glasgow church helped promote the Kentigern legend.

No historian has as yet doubted that Kentigern actually existed, unlike his near-contemporary St Ninian, who recent research has re-cast as a mere mistranscription of history. However the surest fact about Kentigern is his death, which can be pinned down to around 614. Even so, according to one of the two accounts of his life, that made him 185 years old when he died!

In historical reality, Glasgow has no origins legend worth speaking of. Yet the story of its patron saint and his miracles, a mixture of calculated sanctity and fantastic folklore, is acknowledged in the tree, the fish and the ring still represented on the arms of the city. The even more spectacular miracles associated with Kentigern's mother, Thenew (St Enoch), were no barrier to a revival of her legend with the creation of St Enoch Square in the 1780s. Like great nations, great cities need legends. Glasgow has them in abundance.

A greater Glasgow

The milestones to trace the formal foundation of Glasgow are clear enough. The cathedral was first consecrated in 1136 and reconsecrated in 1197, rebuilt after a serious fire in 1189. Both the Glasgow diocese and the parish pre-dated the burgh: the diocese was founded – or refounded – sometime between 1114 and 1118.

Bishops of Glasgow were secular lords as well as princes of the church: their powers, associated with the burgh, originally date from the twelfth century. The cathedral, as a result, acted as the parish church for both the burgh and the surrounding barony, which approximated in area to what is now known as greater Glasgow.

The burgh received its foundation charter as a bishop's burgh sometime between 1175 and 1178, at which time it was granted a weekly market, which took place on Thursdays. It was granted the right to an annual eight-day fair in early July sometime between 1189 and 1198. The 'Glasgow Fair' is its direct successor. Yet Glasgow's pattern of development before 1400 is largely obscure or untraceable; even the sequence of its urban settlement is problematic.

Glasgow's importance within the realm is unclear. It figures little as a place where royal charters were issued. Often, for other burghs, the witnessing of such documents signalled their prominence or significance. Instead, the first traces of Glasgow, as an administrative centre, are firmly linked to its role as the centre of an expanding and ambitious bishopric. Here, there are two key markers, each a papal charter (known as 'bulls').

The bishopric was granted the unusual status of 'special daughter' of Rome, with 'no one in between', in 1175. This accolade underlined Glasgow's position and jurisdiction as separate and independent from the major religious centres of Durham and York. It also gave the city a special status within Scotland, especially in relation to the authority of St Andrews, then the centre for the Scottish church.

Even after Glasgow was raised to the position of Scotland's second archbishopric in 1492 the rivalry between the Glasgow church and St Andrews persisted. In his *History of the Reformation*, John Knox gleefully describes the invasion of Glasgow Cathedral in 1545 by the archbishop of St Andrews and his entire retinue of clergy to try to enforce his superior authority. In Knox's account an unseemly mass brawl ensued at the door of

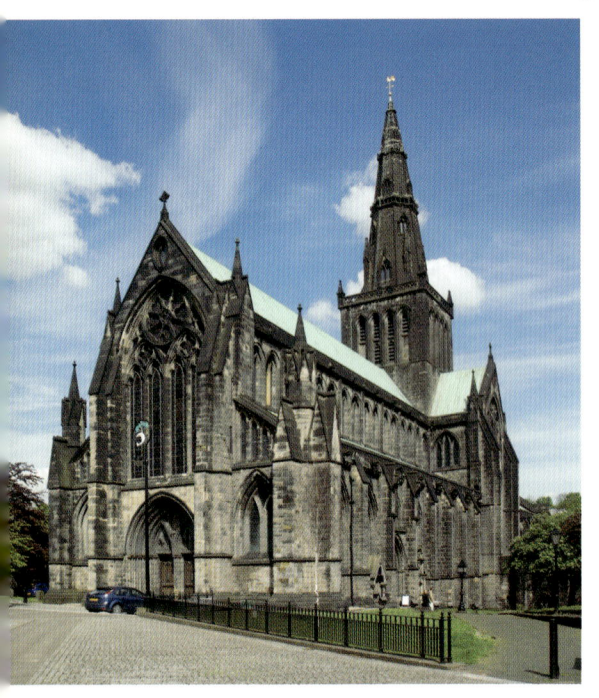

ABOVE
Glasgow Cathedral and Provand's Lordship today

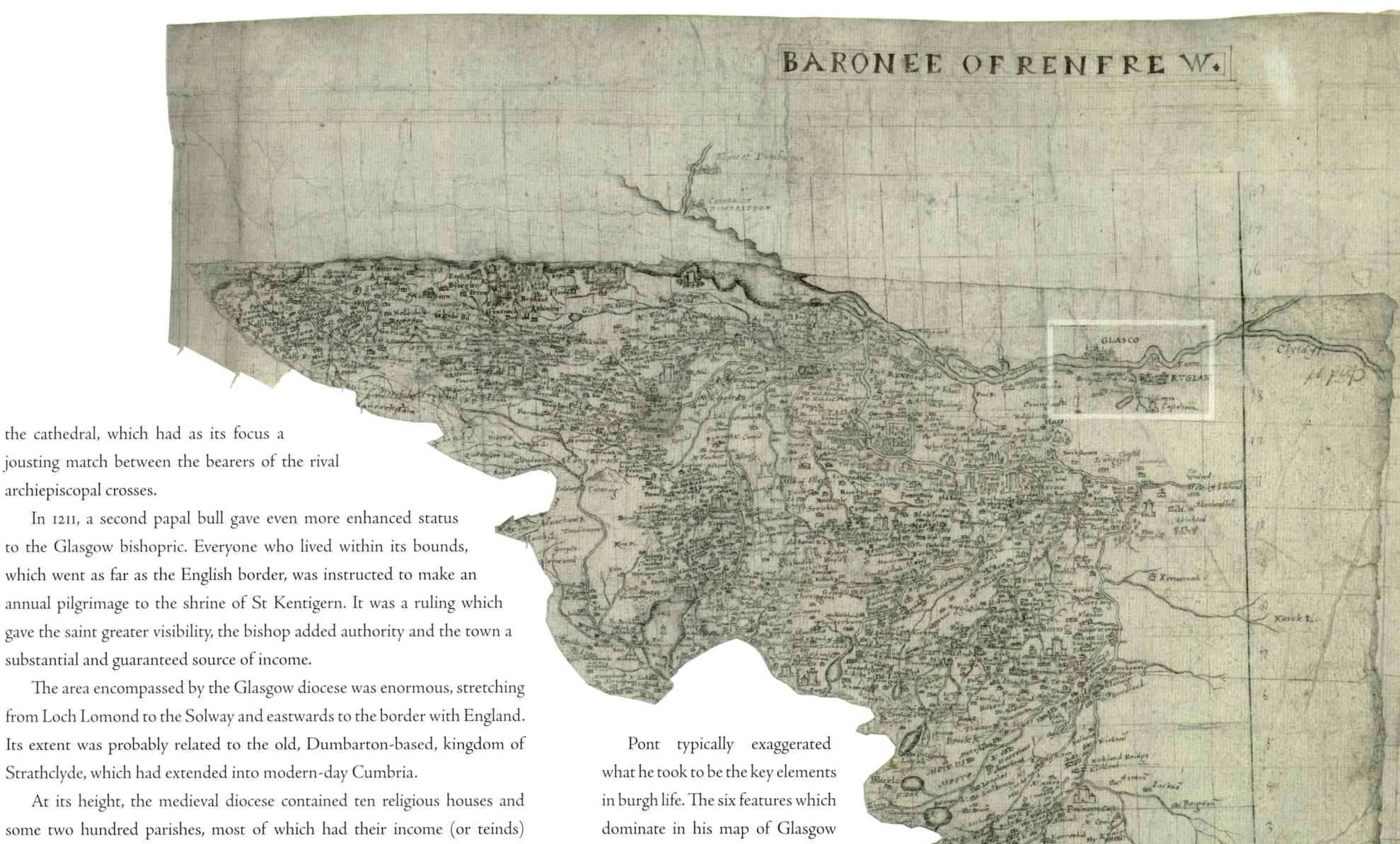

the cathedral, which had as its focus a jousting match between the bearers of the rival archiepiscopal crosses.

In 1211, a second papal bull gave even more enhanced status to the Glasgow bishopric. Everyone who lived within its bounds, which went as far as the English border, was instructed to make an annual pilgrimage to the shrine of St Kentigern. It was a ruling which gave the saint greater visibility, the bishop added authority and the town a substantial and guaranteed source of income.

The area encompassed by the Glasgow diocese was enormous, stretching from Loch Lomond to the Solway and eastwards to the border with England. Its extent was probably related to the old, Dumbarton-based, kingdom of Strathclyde, which had extended into modern-day Cumbria.

At its height, the medieval diocese contained ten religious houses and some two hundred parishes, most of which had their income (or teinds) payable in whole or in part to the bishopric. The size of the barony was no less impressive. Within the barony Glasgow's bishops exercised the full rights of a secular lord, ranging from the right to hold courts to a monopoly of all mills.

The barony stretched as far as the modern city's furthest suburbs, amounting to around seventy square miles. The burgh's common lands were also unusual in both their size and in the income they produced. A rental roll of 1639, recording the income of all the Scottish burghs, placed Glasgow third, after only Edinburgh and Aberdeen. It was little wonder that the hub of Glasgow's diocese boasted the second largest church in the medieval kingdom.

Medieval Glasgow imagined

A GOOD DEAL OF IMAGINATION is needed for the citizen of modern Glasgow to envisage the city or its inhabitants six or seven hundred years ago. Some of the remnants of medieval Glasgow, as they existed in the late seventeenth century, were recorded in the careful sketches drawn by the military engineer, John Slezer. Yet the first authentic glimpse of Glasgow belongs to a century earlier. The extent of its cathedral is clearly portrayed in the first maps of Glasgow, drawn by the cartographer, Timothy Pont, sometime in the late 1580s or the 1590s.

Pont typically exaggerated what he took to be the key elements in burgh life. The six features which dominate in his map of Glasgow are moving, from south to north, its bridge and tolbooth (which predated a new, five-storey building constructed on the same site thirty years later), Glasgow's two friaries, its cathedral and the bishop's castle. It is a remarkable medieval picture of the town.

The origins of the first bridge over the Clyde are unclear. It is first mentioned as late as 1286, more than a century after the formal foundation of the burgh in the 1170s. It is possible that visitors to both the weekly market and the annual fair came by way of a ford a hundred yards upstream from the eventual bridge. At that time the depth of the river at that point would have been a foot or less. The first bridge which may have been a substantially wooden structure, is said to have been replaced by an eight-arch, stone bridge, fully twelve feet (3.6 metres) wide. This impressive structure was in itself a monument to the significance of Glasgow as a trading, administrative and ecclesiastical centre.

The heavy etching on Pont's map of two parallel lines, exaggerating the size of the bridge, revealed how important Pont thought it still was as both a crossing point and an economic conduit. As well as providing a vital passageway for the goods, grain and livestock which flooded into the weekly market and the annual fair, the bridge and ford also provided the means by which the extensive produce of the bishop's lands outside the burgh and barony were transported into the town.

ABOVE
Pont's map of the Barony of Renfrew, c. 1590. Section showing Glasgow highlighted.

GLASGVA
Stoberos
Part of Renfrew
Part of Kunigham
Part of Kyle
Priesthill
Kaldar
Moffat
Krawfurd
HIGGAR
Kilbryde
Loudon

Rents in the middle ages were almost all paid in kind, so cattle, pigs, cheese, butter, malt and grain from estates ranging from Renfrewshire to Galloway and fish caught off the Ayrshire coast, all arrived via the great bridge. The Glasgow market provided the income for the enormous building programme mounted by successive bishops.

The prominence in Pont's map of the Dominican and Franciscan friaries may seem odd, particularly as the cartographer was a Protestant minister's son who followed his father into the ministry. It was nevertheless authentic. Although the houses of the friars were abandoned after 1560, their churches continued in use, the former being absorbed by the growing university and the Franciscan property being rented out. The Observant Franciscans founded their house in the mid 1470s at the edge of the urban settlement. Their church, which had been built as late as 1518-32, needed significant repairs in 1589. The area is now the site of the City Science development, bounded by George Street, Ingram Street and Albion Street.

The upper town

THE SMALLEST OF THE five buildings in Pont's sketch is the bishop's castle. This fortified tower and its associated buildings, first mentioned in the thirteenth century, were located on a site to the west of the cathedral. Surrounded by an early ditch, the castle's ashlar curtain wall was built in the early 1520s. By Pont's time, having been attacked half a dozen times in the course of the sixteenth century, the castle no longer served as a defensible strongpoint.

What needs to be added to this reconstruction of medieval Glasgow is the remainder of the ecclesiastical complex in and around the castle and cathedral. There were four main phases in the long, drawn-out story of the construction of ecclesiastical Glasgow, which probably began sometime in the early twelfth century. The first church was built probably to encase in its crypt an existing shrine dedicated to St Kentigern. The site was awkward, not quite at the apex of a hill and with a steep fall in the ground towards the east, which caused structural problems and necessitated endless repairs throughout the middle ages. It is not known if this first church was fully finished when it was badly damaged by a fire in 1189.

The second stage in the cathedral's history began with the fire and concluded with its formal re-consecration in 1197. A long series of additions and repairs followed, culminating in the last quarter of the fourteenth century, when much of the nave and transepts were built. Even more extensive building work came about during the period of Bishop Matthew Glendinning (1387-1408) after the cathedral was struck by lightning. A new shrine of gold or silver was built to house Kentigern's relics.

The fourth intensive phase of cathedral building came in the fifty years after 1470, when a series of side altars were added as well as the Blacader (often now spelt Blackadder) Aisle, built at the behest of Glasgow's first archbishop, Robert Blacader (1483-1508). This late Gothic marvel took no less than twenty-five years to build.

It is easy to have a static notion of the middle ages. However, for most of the time between when the cathedral was first consecrated in 1136 and the Reformation, upper Glasgow was a very busy building site, with all that that implies in terms of activity, dirt, noise and a sizeable permanent workforce of masons, carpenters and labourers.

There is also much to imagine about Glasgow's medieval people. The population of the upper town may well have had more than one cleric to every forty people. Most of the clerics, and certainly by far the majority of the chaplains and prebendaries, would have been Glasgow-born and bred. The foundation charters of many altars stipulated as much.

Yet the only evidence for modern observers, aside from the cathedral itself, is the surviving building known as Provand's Lordship. This manse, dating from 1471, formed part of a hospital for the poor, dedicated to St Nicholas and founded by 1464. This late date serves as a reminder that Glasgow's 'medieval' church complex was still being added to, virtually right up to the Reformation.

While Provand's Lordship can still be seen, little else remains of the surge of building which accompanied the campaign for Glasgow to be elevated into an archbishopric and the celebration of its new-found status after 1492. No trace remains of Blacader's Hospital, founded about 1524, or of the large collegiate church of St Mary of Loreto and St Anne, founded as late as 1525. Also long gone are the collection of more than half a dozen chapels, like those dedicated to St Ninian and St Roche.

Provand's Lordship is the only reminder of the sprawling complex of stone-built manses occupied by canons of the cathedral which, in both number and extent, must have surpassed their counterparts in any of the other episcopal centres in medieval Scotland. A document in 1258 refers to improving the canons' houses. By 1440 there were thirty-two individual canons' dwellings.

Even topography needs to be re-invented in the mind. The deep course of the Molendinar Burn defined the eastern limits of the episcopal precinct. Although prominently etched on Pont's map of Glasgow, the burn is now culverted and its deep valley flattened beyond recognition.

ABOVE
Etching of the Molendinar Burn, Robert Paul, mid 18th century

OPPOSITE
Pont's map, c. 1590 with digitally-enhanced section showing Glasgow

ABOVE
Stained glass panel containing a hunting scene, huntsman has fishing rod on shoulder, quiver at side. English, 15th century

BELOW RIGHT
Penny, David II, 1357-67

Everyday life

THE LIVES OF ORDINARY Glaswegians are little recorded. Those that can be traced in the records are the burgesses, who held the 'freedom' of the city and made up less than a third of adult males. Freedom, of course, meant privilege. The remaining two thirds were 'unfree', meaning that they held no burgess rights, such as privileged access to the market or common lands.

In an odd inversion of what the present-day observer might expect, the poorer a town dweller was the more jobs he or she was likely to have. A good deal of low-grade employment was casual or seasonal. For most Glaswegians, there would have been little notion of childhood and certainly no concept of retirement.

'Hospitals' in the middle ages were either asylums to keep the disease-ridden safely imprisoned or, for a few of the privileged elite, rest homes in quasi-monastic surroundings. Women faced horrific death rates in childbirth. However if they survived those years they tended to live longer than men.

For the first Glaswegians old age came early, in the forties rather than in the sixties, which very few reached. Most children entered the world of work aged about seven, after a very basic education in an 'Inglis' or vernacular school. Sons of burgesses might continue their education until twelve or thirteen in the Latin world of the grammar school. A few others might be trained in the song school as choristers or, eventually, as clergy. Life was usually short, unrelenting and almost indescribably tough.

A boom town?

THE PERIOD WHICH HAS attracted most attention in Glasgow's pre-modern history has usually been the seventeenth century when, it has been argued, it became a 'boom town'. The real boom in population, however, probably came earlier, between 1450 and 1600. It seems likely that over that period Glasgow's population increased from a little more than a thousand inhabitants to seven or eight times that figure. Although this period saw population expansion everywhere in Scotland, in countryside as well as town, the rate of increase was at its greatest in the larger towns.

In 1636, an English visitor, William Brereton, described Glasgow as having "six or seven thousand communicants and about twenty thousand persons in the town". Population estimates, as with those of crowds, were no more accurate in the seventeenth century than they are in the twenty-first but there is a useful point of comparison. The other town on which Brereton exercised his powers of exaggeration was Edinburgh, where he estimated there were about 16,000 communicants. The standard device for adding in children, by multiplying the figure for adults by a factor of 1.7, indicates that Glasgow was probably somewhere between a third and a half the size of Edinburgh within its walls. In other words, mid-seventeenth century Glasgow had 10,000-12,000 inhabitants.

What was the economic basis for this expansion? One answer lies in Glasgow's steady gain in trade, at the expense of Dumbarton, Renfrew, Rutherglen and Lanark. In 1535, Glasgow accounted for 36 per cent of the taxation levied on these Upper Clyde burghs. By 1594, it contributed over 61 per cent of the region's taxation. By 1635, in national terms, it was ranked fourth equal with Perth, behind only Edinburgh, Dundee and Aberdeen.

Contrary to what might be expected, this expansion was not through overseas trade. Much of Glasgow's exports were still routed through the Forth ports of Bo'ness and Blackness, at the end of a tortuous overland trek. Glasgow's success came much more through an increasing domination of inland and regional trade at the expense of its neighbours.

Yet the figures for burgh taxation crucially underestimate Glasgow's income. They represent a measure of the burgh's income, mostly from trade of one sort or another. They would not have reflected the pre-Reformation income of the bishopric, which must have been enormous and much of which was probably paid in kind.

The bishopric's income was mostly ploughed back into a prestigious building programme within the bishop's burgh. The produce and livestock from rents and teinds paid in kind must have been circulated via the burgh's marketplace. As a result, the size and wealth of medieval Glasgow, the largest town in Scotland which was the centre of a bishopric, must have been distinctly larger than the burgh taxation figures indicate. Glasgow was a centre of very conspicuous consumption.

The market and trade

Glasgow features in three of Pont's maps. The key point in the most revealing of the three is the exaggerated depiction of the bridge over the Clyde. In other words, both before and after the Reformation, Glasgow was expanding rapidly as a market centre for a large part of the old diocese to the south of the river and for much of the hinterland immediately to the north and west of the Clyde. After the Reformation in 1560 there is no hint of economic collapse or even stagnation, as happened in some episcopal centres in England and Europe.

Glasgow's population continued to grow, as did the burgh economy. An increase in the city's industry served as a substitute wealth creator. Ever greater numbers of hucksters, packmen and travellers selling their wares replaced Glasgow's former reliance on throngs of medieval pilgrims in their annual trek from all corners of the diocese.

A market centre comprised much more than a mere marketplace. It was also an industrial complex. The point is established by a list of members of the merchant guildry recorded in 1605. Guild members, who enjoyed a privileged status, setting them above ordinary burgesses, included both merchants *and* craftsmen. To qualify, they had to be employers of labour who did not themselves work with their hands.

Glasgow had 213 merchants, who would have ranged from a handful of overseas traders to a phalanx of shopkeepers, booth owners (called cramers) and market traders. But, more significantly, it also had 361 master craftsmen, with a particularly large number of tailors (65), alongside 55 maltsters, 50 cordiners (or shoemakers), 30 weavers, 27 hammermen (or metalworkers) and 27 baxters (or bakers). This was a town which was dominated by three sectors: textiles, manufacture and the food and drink trades.

It has been claimed that Glasgow was different from other large towns, having a freer atmosphere for the economy to develop. It is certainly true that it had a quite different social structure from the larger towns which were also sea ports, such as Aberdeen and Dundee. Yet in this period Glasgow would have looked very like Perth, another craftsman's town, also at the centre of a large rural hinterland. It supplied the countryside around with manufactured goods and drew upon it for raw materials, partly made-up goods and seasonal labour.

In towns like Glasgow would be found the finishing processes for domestic rural textiles in the shape of weavers, dyers, tailors, bonnetmakers and the like. Alongside the clothing trade were the primitive industrial processes which formed the core of the leather and metal trades. This resulted in a concentration of skinners, glovers, cordiners, tanners, and various kinds of metal workers, ranging from smiths to locksmiths and pewterers.

Whatever view we might take of the drinking capacity of Glaswegians, it is striking that the second largest occupation in 1605, after tailors, was that of maltsters, whose numbers were twice as large as the bakers. This suggests three things: that Glasgow was a centre for ale production with customers far beyond the precincts of the town; it had a sizeable number of malt barns, drying kilns and vats which must have been on a quasi-industrial scale; and that this brewing complex must have been located near a readily available water supply.

The water was most probably provided to the east end of the town, near the Molendinar Burn. Drink, it seems, was Glasgow's first and foremost industry by the end of the middle ages.

Growth and change

By 1600 or thereabouts, the bishop's burgh which had been dominated for most of the middle ages by the bishop's castle and the cathedral complex – symbols of power and a generator of income from endless queues of pilgrims – had been transformed into a town with a thoroughly diversified industrial and trading economy.

Kentigern's shrine never featured in the travel brochures for long-distance English and continental pilgrims in the way that St Andrews, with its biblical saint, undoubtedly did. However, Glasgow probably rivalled St Andrews and Dunfermline for the position of the main pilgrimage centre in late medieval Scotland. Visitor numbers would have been swollen by the required annual visit to the shrine by all the adult inhabitants of the diocese.

The reasons for Glasgow's transition from an ecclesiastical honey-pot to the fourth or fifth largest urban settlement in Scotland remain something of a mystery. The answer does not lie, as is so often assumed, in the seventeenth century. Medieval Glasgow was a boom town. Its remarkable growth needs to be understood and explained in the context of the one hundred and fifty years following the foundation of the university in 1451.

A flurry of ecclesiastical building had taken place from the 1430s onwards, including additions to the canons' manses around the cathedral. A further surge took place after 1470. It included the chapel and hospital dedicated to St Nicholas, extensions to the cathedral such as the Blacader Aisle, and the new Franciscan friary. That surge became a flood in the first quarter of the sixteenth century, including new chapels dedicated to St Kentigern and St Roche, an extended friary church and a new collegiate church.

More and more, though, the key to Glasgow's growth in the period between 1450 and 1600 was its bridge, linking its hinterlands to a thriving market place. There are a number of clues as to the expansion of the market town. All references to its gates (or ports) belong to either the fifteenth or sixteenth centuries, which suggests significant growth during that period. There are further references to some ports, like that at the Trongate or West Port, being moved. Trongate shifted in 1588, the same year in which a new gate, Lindsay's Port, was first mentioned. This was set at the end of a new street, the Old Wynd, first laid out in 1573.

In its early history, Glasgow had only one marketplace, a privilege granted to it by the crown in the 1170s. At that point, it is likely that this market was located in the upper town, just to the south of the cathedral. When this market was transferred to the lower town is unclear, but it had certainly been relocated by the fourteenth century.

By the sixteenth century, a series of specialist markets had developed, opening on different days of the week and sited in different parts of the town. The market for woollen cloth and linen was located around the market cross and that for fruit and vegetables was in the Gallowgate. Other markets were set up nearby: the meal market was in the yard of the old Blackfriars; the horse market stood opposite, on the other side of the High Street. The grassmarket, where produce from the surrounding countryside was sold, was beside the Tron and the new Tron Church after 1599. The fish market, for obvious reasons, was placed at the edge of town, at the West Port.

This process, of trade expansion being reflected in the physical layout of the town, continued as the seventeenth century progressed. The replacement of some old street names, such as St Thenew's Gate being renamed Trongate, also reflected the shifting locations of some of the town's industries.

There were other signs of expansion. The foundation, in the nucleus of the market town, of two new churches in the 1520s and 1530s strongly suggests a growing population. The collegiate church of St Mary of Loreto and St Anne had a complement of a provost, no fewer than nine clerics and three choristers. It must have been sizeable, although no physical trace of it now exists on the footprint of the later Tron Kirk, now the site of the Tron Theatre, in the Trongate.

This substantial new church was required to supplement the old arrangement whereby the nave of the cathedral acted as the parish church of the burgh, and to do so in a more convenient place, closer to the economic hub of the market. The extended church provided by the Observant Franciscans hints at the need of local people for the ministrations of an order of friars which specialised as confessors and providers of alms for the poor.

New wells, such as that dug in Gallowgate in 1575, suggest a build-up of population in particular areas, mostly around the market cross. Another sign of the growing pressure on the water supply, caused both by a swelling population and the increasing demands of industry, was the state of some of the streams which ran along the eastern edge of the town. Many of the finishing processes associated with the wool and leather trades were based on the Molendinar Burn.

It is likely that waulk or fulling mills were concentrated at the junction of the Molendinar and Camlachie burns, a few metres north of the river, where the burns curved towards the south-east corner of settlement. The 'Vico Fullorum' (the street of the fullers) was mentioned in the town's records in 1447 and 'Walcargate' in 1454.

BELOW
Extract from Blaeu's map, 1654

The final chapter?

When should the story of medieval Glasgow be brought to an end? There is more than one possibility. The most obvious and yet the most superficial of dates would be 1560 and the acceptance of the Protestant Reformation by the Scottish Parliament. This prompted the flight of James Beaton, Glasgow's last pre-Reformation Catholic archbishop and chancellor of its university, into exile in France.

On the face of it, the Protestant revolution brought to an end a succession of bishops going back to the first recorded incumbent, Michael, in 1109. Yet Glasgow continued to be run like a bishop's burgh for a considerable time after 1560. The return, in controversial circumstances, of a Protestant archbishop in 1573 restored the web of episcopal jurisdictions built up over centuries. However the income of the bishopric was now drastically reduced by the on-going process of the feuing of kirklands.

The power and presence of Glasgow's bishops and archbishops were restored until December 1638, when the incumbent, Patrick Lindsay, was forced to take refuge, along with two fellow bishops, in his castle. What is sometimes called Scotland's second Protestant Reformation had its focus in the meeting of the General Assembly at Glasgow which abolished episcopacy. Although bishops returned to both Glasgow and Scotland in 1661 after the Restoration of Charles II (1651-85), they were a shadow of their former selves.

If 1638 marks one ending, in the form of the effective demise of episcopal control over the burgh, a series of more positive signs can be detected a generation or so before that. One of Pont's maps of Glasgow, dated to 1596, shows a town almost bursting at its seams. The simple medieval cruciform street pattern has expanded into a shape like an evenly balanced cross of Lorraine. The two (double) crosses in this plan are formed by the junctions of the High Street and Bridgegate with Trongate and Gallowgate to the south and with Rottenrow and Drygate nearer to the cathedral in the north.

What is also clear from Pont's drawing is that the outline pattern was becoming studded with backlands and filled in by a welter of adjoining burgage plots. Along Rottenrow, a cluster of new suburbs appeared, close to the site of the old Franciscan friary which, when it was built in the 1470s, had been outside the town.

The precise rate of growth of the town is difficult to pin down with precision. However if there was a single moment which brought to an end the centuries-old notion of a single burgh community, which worshipped as a united body or *corpus christianum*, it came in 1596. The impetus may have come from outwith Glasgow. In that year the Convention of Royal Burghs recommended that every large burgh should sub-divide its parish. As such, Glasgow joined the ranks of what since the fourteenth century had been termed 'the four great towns of Scotland' – Aberdeen, Dundee, Edinburgh and Perth.

Dundee and Perth resolved the dilemma of a growing population overcrowding the burgh church by the creation of a kind of team ministry. Glasgow, like Aberdeen, went for a simpler solution. It decided to create a

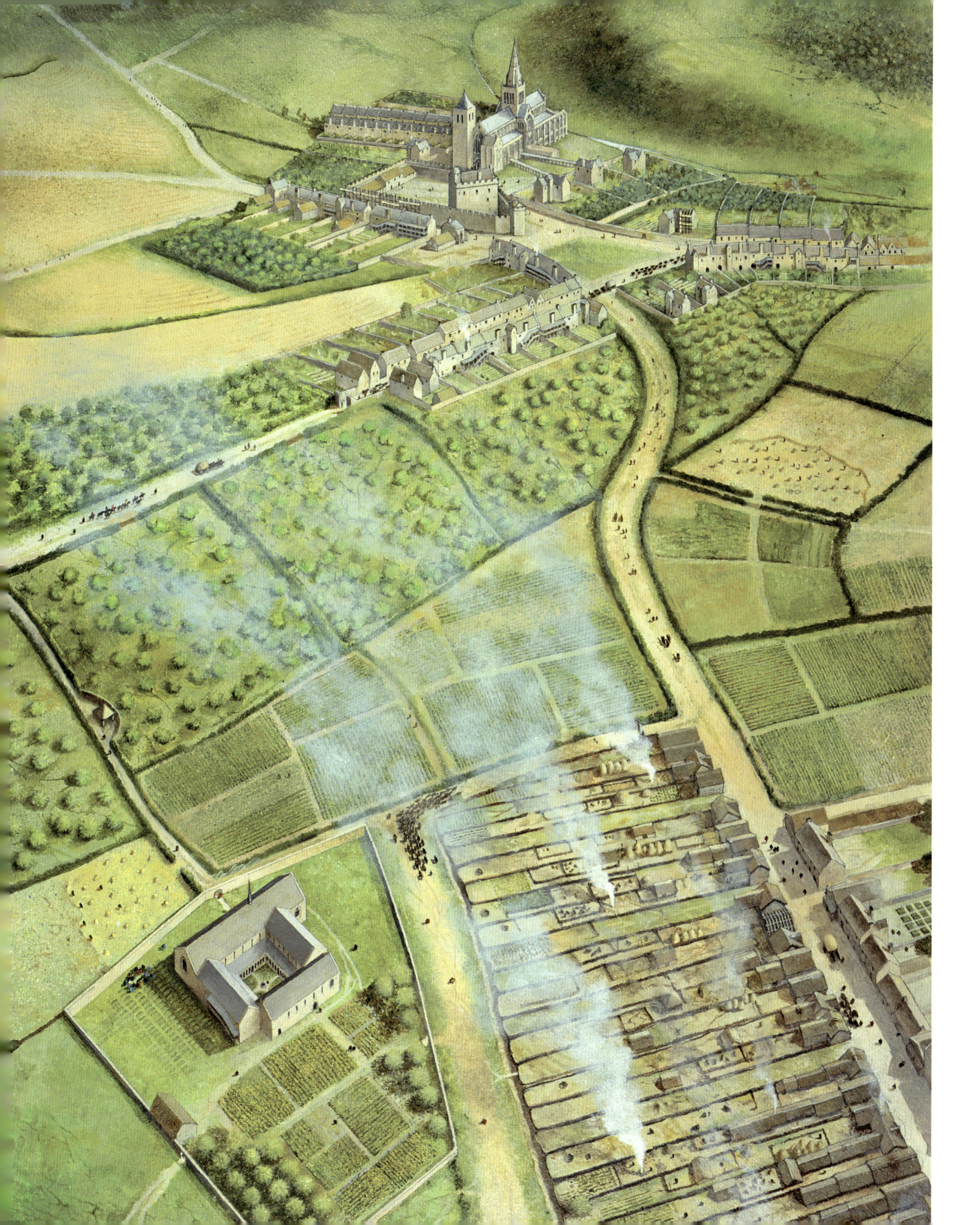

LEFT
Medieval High Street c. 1520. Watercolour illustration by David Simon, 2006.

17

second parish, with its own church. This was the Tron Kirk, built beside the public weighbeam or tron. This new church came into use in 1599.

Even so, the need for a second parish church, adjacent to the burgh's central market, had already been anticipated before the Reformation. The loss of the collegiate church of St Mary of Loreto and St Anne, described in 1570 as 'destroyed and thrown down', had made the crisis of church provision more pressing. The expanding population was increasingly located in and around the Tron and market cross. The Tron Kirk, on the site of the old collegiate church, was built to answer this problem.

Like much else in Glasgow's roll call of great institutions, the university was a medieval foundation. Like Scotland's other ancient seats of learning, St Andrews and Aberdeen, it was the creation of a bishop. The university was deeply tied in with the ambitions of the archbishopric. As early as the 1490s it was described as being a 'metropolitan university'. It shared in the flurry of ecclesiastical building which marked the first quarter of the sixteenth century. Yet, at the time of the flight of its last Catholic chancellor into exile in 1560, it seemed moribund with only two members of staff and no students.

Civic ambition quickly replaced that of Glasgow's medieval archbishops. In 1573, after the troubled decade that followed the Reformation and the civil war that ensued after the deposing of Mary, Queen of Scots was past, the burgh council set out plans to reform 'our pedagogy of Glasgow'. Yet little was new, either in the curriculum, still dominated by philosophy and theology, or in the monastic-style discipline inflicted on both students and staff. Wives were grudgingly allowed only if teachers 'be not able to bear the life of chastity and cannot contain themselves', but staff were obliged to live in college and wives had to keep away from the campus.

Yet the changes and a fresh injection of finance quickly took effect. By the 1580s, about eleven students matriculated each year. This rose to nineteen a year in the 1590s, over thirty a year in the 1620s and about forty a year in the early 1630s. These statistics help explain the building programme on which the university embarked after 1630, on a new site to the east of the High Street. These numbers, however, only include those who matriculated. Many others came and went to classes with no intention of sitting examinations and without bothering to register formally.

Most of these students were only in their early teens, starting their studies at the age of thirteen or so. As student numbers increased, many of them would have had to live in lodgings in the town because of lack of accommodation in the college itself. An unregimented tribe of teenagers must have worried burgh authorities, already concerned with how to police a growing population and a largely mobile workforce.

With urban growth went further civic ambition. A new tolbooth was built around 1626, a remarkable five storeys high and five bays wide. Only its steeple remains today. The High Street was broadened in 1628; new wells were dug in the 1620s and 1630s; and the steeple on the Tron Kirk was substantially altered between 1630 and 1636. The speed of change from medieval bishop's burgh to a new town anxious to forge a new image of itself quickened with each decade in the first half of the seventeenth century.

The end of an era

Glasgow's growth accelerated still further as a direct result of the severe fire of 1652, which engulfed much of the spider's web of alleys and closes off the Saltmarket and Trongate. Contemporary accounts bemoaned the loss of 'foir scoir closes all burnt, estimate to about a thousand families' and eighty warehouses. These reports almost certainly exaggerated the extent of the fire but testified at the same time to the uncontrolled growth of the late medieval town. This settlement had been characterised by the close-packed layout of housing, the use of timber as the main construction material and the combustible nature of storage material, which probably included miniature mountains of hay and malt.

In the aftermath of the 1652 fire, the largely unplanned shambles which had grown up since the thirteenth century along the medieval town's main roadway to its bridge was replaced. A new quarter of houses and warehouses grew up. They were built partly of stone rather than wholly of wood as before and were laid out in a more carefully planned street pattern, without overhanging upper storeys and garrets. All houses on both sides of the Saltmarket were to be built to 'conforme to ane straicht lyne, and none to come fader then another'. This new precinct lasted until it, in turn, became a slum. Most of these dwellings were demolished in the late nineteenth century after the City Improvement Act of 1866.

The great fire of Glasgow of 1652 provides a fitting point to bring to an end the story of medieval Glasgow. The 'middle ages' lasted a very long time – longer than the period which separates the present day from the century of the Reformation. The term, middle ages, was the creation of a generation of intellectuals which first detected in the 1490s something different about the spirit of the age in which they lived. It is useful, but only up to a point.

What can be said of the preoccupations, fears and obsessions of Glaswegians at the end of the middle ages? What were the thoughts of the queues of pilgrims winding their way through the cathedral, shepherded by stewards to reach the shrine of St Kentigern at the precise time of the day when the light hit the tomb? This daily ritual had been going on for centuries.

Pilgrimage was a way of life but pilgrimage junkies were probably less prominent by 1500 than they had been in 1300 or 1400. The dedication of a new altar to Kentigern within the cathedral in 1460 and a new chapel to the Saint being founded in 1500, give no hint of the waning of his cult. However fashions in piety did change over time.

The foundation of three churches in the early years of the sixteenth century testifies to Glasgow's change of mood. The formalities which marked the endowment of the chapel of St Roche in 1508 attracted 'a great and overflowing multitude and numbers in the tolbooth'. The cult of this hermit, who had spent most of his life on pilgrimage, is a sure sign of the renewed fear of the plague which swept across society from the 1490s onwards in a series of minor epidemics. None matched the toll wreaked by the Black Death of 1349, when one in three of the canons of St Andrews died, but the plague, often the mask for other diseases such as typhoid or cholera, was largely an urban disease, provoked by overcrowding and poor sanitation.

The basic purpose of the substantial collegiate church built in the Trongate in the 1520s, a kind of surrogate second parish church, was to say masses for the souls of the dead. A staff of twelve and seven separate altars would have meant that there would not have been a daylight hour when a votive mass for the dead was not being celebrated. Almost all the chaplains were locals, the sons of burgesses 'learned and meet'. The choice of saintly intercessors is often significant. The dedications in this church – to St Anne, mother of Mary, as well as the Virgin herself – strongly suggest a dedicated female clientele as well as a male one.

The enlarging of the nearby Franciscan church attests to the number of legacies given to a strict mendicant order. The Franciscans were much in demand because of their licence to hear death-bed confessions and to permit burial of ordinary members of society within their own kirkyard as lay brothers or sisters. All three of these new church foundations demonstrate how much the fear of death and an obsession with the after-life dominated the medieval mind.

For Glaswegians, these thoughts and fears went on, regardless of seismic events in religion and politics. Aside from the change of religion which they experienced in and after the Reformation of 1560, the disappearance of some of the town's religious places and the advent of new ones, the rest of life – whether industry, trade, housing, health or disease – all suggested that the more that things changed, the more they generally stayed the same, at least until the second half of the seventeenth century.

The day-to-day experience of the people of Glasgow during the first centuries of the town is a reality which defies simple descriptions and the standard terms for historical periods used by historians. For its ordinary citizens, medieval Glasgow persisted a century or more after most textbooks tell us that the 'middle ages' had come to an end.

LEFT
Glasgow Cathedral from Mason Street. Watercolour by A D Robertson, 1840.

OPPOSITE
Stained glass medallion with floral ornament in the form of a white tree with five branches. English, 14th century.

Stained glass medallion with grotesque figure, half human with jester's hood and cape, half goat-like creature. English, 14th century.

Glasgow, which took root among them, has grown, flourished and

endured

Greater Glasgow

NORMAN F SHEAD

A confusion of kingdoms

IN THE LATE SIXTH CENTURY when St Kentigern (Mungo) came to 'Cathures which is now called Glasgow' (as his twelfth century biographer tells us), Scotland was much divided. Politically there were several kingdoms, whose precise boundaries cannot be traced, partly because they changed considerably over time. In addition, Scotland was divided by language.

Kentigern was in that part of Scotland where Cumbric (something like Welsh) was spoken. It was divided into kingdoms: the best known are that of the Gododdin in the centre and east based on the rock of Edinburgh. The kingdom of Manau was centred on the rock of Stirling. Rheged straddled the later Anglo-Scottish border, and the kingdom of Dumbarton was based on the rock of the same name.

In the south-east the stronghold of the Angles of Bernicia, was Bamburgh. These people may have been descendants of Germanic soldiers garrisoning Hadrian's Wall. It seems likely that the Cumbric-speaking population was ruled by an aristocracy who spoke Anglo-Saxon. Their rule eventually extended to the Forth, including Edinburgh.

To the north dwelt the Picts, whose language was also related to Welsh. Pictish speakers lived in what would later become Scotia, that is Scotland north of the River Forth. They were not always united in one kingdom. To the west was the Gaelic-speaking kingdom of Dalriada, occupying roughly modern Argyll.

These complex political arrangements were subject to change, usually violent. That included the arrival of the Vikings, first as raiders at the end of the eighth century (Iona was plundered in 802) and then as settlers in Northern Scotland and the Northern and Western Isles. The Viking presence may have played some part in the most significant development of all: the union of Picts and Scots. Exactly how that union came about is far from clear. However one consequence was the disappearance of the Pictish language.

The Northumbrians extended their rule across the Forth for a time, but were defeated by the Picts at Dunnichen (Nechtansmere) in 685, and driven back to the Forth. By the tenth century the kings of Scots were gradually extending their power into Lothian. In the early 970s the Anglo-Saxon King Edgar granted Lothian to the king of Scots, Kenneth II, a change confirmed by Malcolm II's victory over the earl of Northumbria at the battle of Carham (1018).

The Gododdin were probably much weakened, perhaps fatally, by defeat at Catterick. This important battle, which is known from the ancient poem *The Gododdin*, took place in Kentigern's lifetime. The British kingdoms within Scotland were gradually reduced to one, Cumbria (called Strathclyde by the English), an enlargement of the former kingdom of Dumbarton. Again, it would be impossible to map Cumbria with any accuracy. At times it extended south into modern England, but was subject to periods of contraction.

In the early eighth century the Angles invaded Galloway and were sufficiently firmly established to create a bishopric at Whithorn which lasted for about a century with a succession of five or six bishops. At the height of their power they also spread into Ayrshire. The kingdom suffered a major disaster in 870 when the fort on Dumbarton Rock was destroyed after a siege by Vikings from Dublin who carried off the king to Ireland. Nonetheless a native dynasty survived until the eleventh century. The last certain Cumbrian king was Owen the Bald, who fought as an ally of the king of Scots at Carham. Between 1018 and 1054 there is no certain information about Cumbria.

An attack in 1030 by the English and by Scandinavians from Dublin may well have been against the Cumbrians. That might explain the collapse of the kingdom, and it seems possible that the king of Scots might have acquired some control over Cumbria as a result of these events.

In 1054 Earl Siward of Northumbria invaded, defeated King Macbeth and put King Malcolm on the throne. Described as 'son of the king of the Cumbrians', Malcolm may well have been a son or grandson of Owen. As the throne in question was not that of Scotia, for Macbeth was not overthrown for that prize till 1057, it seems likely to be that of Cumbria. Between then and 1107 there is again a blank period.

When Cumbria next appears, it is as a bequest by King Edgar to his youngest brother David (the future King David I), the crown passing in the interim to their brother Alexander I (1107-1124). David had spent many years in England. He was of some eminence at the court of Henry I, (who had married David's sister). David's claim to Cumbria seems to have been resisted by Alexander. Perhaps David had the backing of Henry I in securing it. With David's accession to the Scottish throne in 1124 Cumbria became one of the possessions of the Scottish crown.

These changes in rule and shifts in power over Scotland's early centuries are extraordinarily complex. In such a brief summary they are undoubtedly confusing. Yet this was the political landscape within which the town which would, in time become the great city of Glasgow came into being. All these ancient kingdoms are now merely places of memory. Yet Glasgow, which took root among them, has grown, flourished and endured.

Glasgow's rural setting

MEDIEVAL GLASGOW WAS SET in a rural landscape. Most of the population of the diocese lived in touns or townships, which probably consisted of twenty to thirty houses, or in hamlets of five to twelve households. The houses were built of timber or on timber frames supporting turves or rubble. One end of the house was often used to house the most valuable beasts.

By the fifteenth century, and probably long before, arable land was described as 'infield' and 'outfield'. The infield was intensively cultivated; the outfield, poorer quality land, was only partially cultivated. The land was

RIGHT
ollam righ Alban inagurating Alexander III from a late medieval manuscript

BELOW
Indicative plan – the ancient kingdoms of Scotland, c. 600AD

divided into strips; one man's strips would be scattered about the area, not in a compact block. Ploughing was probably done with a team of oxen, though mixed teams of oxen and horses were also possible. Opening up new land to cultivation was called assarting.

Wheat was relatively rare. The lack of Scottish supplies led Kilwinning Abbey to buy grain from Ireland in the 1220s. The main crops were oats and barley with kail, peas and beans also being grown. People kept cattle and flocks of sheep. David I granted Glasgow Cathedral a tenth of his cattle and swine in Renfrewshire and Ayrshire.

There were fisheries in the Clyde and on the coast. The monks of Melrose were given a fishery and salt pans on the Ayrshire coast (salt was essential to preserve food), and managed their Ayrshire properties from Mauchline, which seems to have operated as a grange (an outlying economic centre for monasteries). Grangehill by Beith and Grange, both in Ayrshire, seem to preserve the memory of granges of Kilwinning and Melrose Abbeys.

In the thirteenth century butter, cheese, oatmeal, barley, malt, cattle, pigs, eels, salmon, herring and venison were used in the payment of rents. In 1227 the Earl of Lennox promised to pay in full the teinds (a payment to the Church, nominally a tenth of a person's wealth) due to Glasgow Cathedral in grain, hay, wool, flax, cheese, butter, calves, lambs, pigs, foals and goats.

The estates of great lords, including the bishop, were also not in compact blocks; the land worked directly for the lord was the demesne (the root of the later word 'mains'). There were also forests (which were hunting areas, not simply tree covered landscape). The bishops forest was famous enough to be mentioned in the late twelfth century poem *Fergus of Galloway*.

The later middle ages saw many changes. There is no evidence to show what effect the great famine of 1315-16, the Black Death and the long Anglo-Scottish wars had on the population of the Glasgow diocese. The plague generally made it difficult to find tenants, and labour costs rose. Serfdom died out, but there continued to be different ranks among the peasantry. Demesnes were rented out to tenants, for it became easier to collect rents than to hire labour.

From about 1500 feus, which gave security of tenure for a fixed rent, were common, especially on the lands of the king and the Church. A rental book for part of the Glasgow diocese, covering the years from 1509 to the Protestant Reformation survives. The burgesses of Glasgow had arable land cultivated by the freemen, and common land provided peat, wood and stone and pasture for cattle.

St. Kentigern

Very little is known with certainty about Kentigern. Two lifes of the Saint were written in the twelfth century. The first commissioned by Bishop Herbert (1147-1164) is incomplete. The other, *Kentigern: De Vita Sua*, was commissioned by Bishop Jocelin (1175-1199) and was penned by his namesake, Jocelin of Furness, author of other saints' lives and, like the bishop, a Cistercian monk. The records which contributed to the latter account may go back to the late seventh or early eighth century, about a century after Kentigern's death. The king of Dumbarton, Rhydderch Hael, who is said in the book to have been the saint's contemporary, is a historical figure who died about 614.

An early date for some of the information in the *Life of Kentigern* is suggested by references to ecclesiastical practices which had long been in disuse by the twelfth century. These included the consecration of a bishop by only one other rather than three, and the custom of baptizing at Epiphany.

What can be said with confidence about Kentigern's career is slight. It seems likely that Christianity already existed in the kingdom of Dumbarton before his arrival, but it is not certain how widespread it was. His name is British, he seems to have been bishop of the kingdom of Dumbarton during the reign of Rhydderch Hael. He may have been head of a community, though probably of clergy rather than monks (the *Life* speaks of his disciples), and he died about 613 or 614, the only fact for which there is corroboration (in the Welsh Annals).

ABOVE
Page from the Life of Kentigern

ABOVE
Archbishop Robert Blacader window, Glasgow Cathedral, by Harry Stammers, 1961

Developing the diocese

BY THE TWELFTH CENTURY Kentigern was regarded as the first bishop of Glasgow, though there is no evidence of successors until the eleventh century. It is, however, unlikely that a Christian kingdom would have no bishop of its own. The cathedral, built by Bishop John in the twelfth century, was awkwardly situated near the Molendinar Burn and not even on the highest point in the area. It has to be assumed that this was believed to be the site of Kentigern's church.

The well, built into the fabric of the third cathedral, was presumably thought to be the Saint's. David, as ruler of Cumbria, had a survey made of the lands belonging to Glasgow. This was recorded in writing at some time between 1114 and 1124, though the actual enquiry may have been at a slightly earlier date.

David's survey covered each province of Cumbria which he ruled 'for he did not rule the whole of Cumbria'. The place names in David's report are all in modern Scotland. The absence of names from modern England probably resulted from changes brought about by King William II. In 1092 William had driven out the ruler of Cumberland, built a castle at Carlisle, revived the city and brought peasants to colonize the area. At least David's survey shows that it was believed that a diocese of Glasgow had existed and that its property could be identified.

In the early twelfth century a writer in York claimed that the archbishop of York had consecrated two bishops of Glasgow in the late 1050s. There is no other record of this claim and it looks like a clumsy attempt to assert York's authority over the bishop of Glasgow, and perhaps the other Scottish bishops, at a time when this was a burning issue.

Another bishop known only from York sources is Michael. Described as a 'Briton', he is said to have been appointed as Bishop of Glasgow by David and consecrated by the archbishop of York. He was buried at Morland in Cumberland and is not known ever to have visited Glasgow. Michael too, might be a York invention, but a copy of his profession of obedience to the archbishop of York survives. This too could be dismissed as York propaganda, but professions of obedience were not invented for other bishops over whom the archbishop claimed authority. As David was not on good terms with his brother, King Alexander I, he may have had no objection to the consecration of Glasgow's bishop by York.

While the claim of Bishop Michael is questionable there is no doubt over David's 'second bishop of Glasgow' John, who had been his tutor. He was consecrated in Rome by Pope Paschal II. Archbishop Thurstan of York later claimed that he had requested the consecration. However consecration by the pope allowed John to avoid a profession of obedience to the archbishop. His successors, Bishop Herbert (1147-1164) and Bishop Ingram (1164-1174) were also both consecrated by popes, Herbert by Eugenius III at Auxerre and Ingram by Alexander III at Sens. Bishop Jocelin (1175-1199) was consecrated by a papal legate, Eskil, Archbishop of Lund, at Clairvaux and Bishop William Malveisin (1200-1202) by the archbishop of Lyons at Lyons, on the authority of Pope Innocent III.

For much of the twelfth century successive popes supported the claims of York over the Scottish bishops. As early as 1100 Paschal II had commanded the suffragans of York throughout Scotia to obey the archbishop. Seventeen papal letters survive on this subject. However by 1200 the archbishop of York had long ago lost any hope of establishing his authority over the bishop of Glasgow and the other Scottish bishops, and Bishop Walter de St Albans (1208-1232) was consecrated at Glasgow by Scottish bishops.

In the first half of the twelfth century, Glasgow could be described as neither in England nor in Scotland. It was described in this way by one archbishop of Canterbury, but he too wanted authority over the bishop of Glasgow. Nonetheless the clergy of Glasgow promoted this unique status, seeing the diocese of Glasgow as the remnant and last survivor of the old kingdom of Cumbria. In 1164, Archdeacon Ingram (the future bishop) and Salomon, the dean of Glasgow Cathedral, opposed the claims of the archbishop of York to his face at Norham, as did Bishop Jocelin in 1176 at a meeting of the English royal council at Northampton.

Jocelin obtained a papal exemption from the authority of any bishop or archbishop, which safeguarded him too from the claims of the bishop of St Andrews as 'bishop of the Scots'. The pope had also declared the church of Glasgow to be 'our special daughter' with 'no one in between', a special status not applied to the whole Scottish Church (excluding Galloway) until around 1189.

The Fourth Lateran Council of 1215 decreed that archbishops were to hold annual councils of their bishops. As the pope could not be expected to do this in Scotland, the Scottish bishops were authorised in 1225 to set up their own council. Membership of this council was wider than the bishops alone, but one of them acted as Conservator or chairman.

In 1472 the bishop of St Andrews was made an archbishop. Glasgow followed in 1492. Bishop Robert Blacader had already been granted exemption from the jurisdiction of St Andrews by the pope and his promotion to the rank of archbishop led to friction between Glasgow and St Andrews from time to time. Glasgow was given the dioceses of Dunkeld, Dunblane, Galloway and Argyll as its subordinates, but Dunblane was given to St Andrews in 1500 and Dunkeld by 1515.

Organising the cathedral

DAVID'S SURVEY OF THE EARLY twelfth century was followed by the construction of Glasgow's first cathedral and the building up of a body of clergy to serve it. The canons who formed the staff of the cathedral had to be supported by the founding of prebends, that is, sources of revenue, usually churches, of which the canons would technically be rectors, for example Govan and Renfrew.

Between them Bishops John and Herbert created seven prebends and Bishop Jocelin added an eighth. Herbert adopted the 'customs' of Salisbury Cathedral as a constitution. The precise nature of these customs is uncertain, but the canons were now a corporate body, the 'chapter'. Glasgow's chapter is first mentioned in a document in 1161 and had its own seal before the end of the century. The earliest dignitary to appear was the archdeacon in the 1120s. At that date the archdeacon was more likely to have assisted the bishop in the administration of the diocese, especially during John's absences. However as no dean is mentioned before 1161, the archdeacon may also have been the president of the chapter until then.

A treasurer, concerned with the ornaments and treasures of the cathedral and the provision of items needed for worship, was in office by the 1190s, as probably was a precentor, in charge of the choir. A chancellor is first mentioned between 1249 and 1258. His duties included direction of a cathedral school, though there is no record of one until the fifteenth century, keeping the chapter's seal and dealing with its correspondence. A sub-dean to deputize for the dean was in office by 1266, but the other deputy, the succentor, is not mentioned until the later 1450s.

By 1248 there were fourteen prebends, by 1325 sixteen and by 1401 twenty-three. A big increase occurred about 1430 with the endowment of seven more, a development perhaps prompted by Bishop John Cameron. By the late fifteenth century the chapter of Glasgow Cathedral consisted of four dignitaries, two archdeacons and twenty-six canons, giving thirty-two prebends in all, the final figure.

The bishop was patron of the canonries. In 1258 Bishop William de Bondington granted the canons the right to elect the dean, and also granted them the fully developed constitution of Salisbury Cathedral. In addition to the canons there were the vicars choral, who deputized for the canons (who were often absent) in singing the daily services. In 1200 the vicars choral were firmly put in their place by Bishop William Malveisin, who told them that they had no voice in the chapter and no right to take part in the election of the bishop. They were, however, constituted as a college by Bishop Andrew de Durisdeer (1455-1473), who provided them with their own hall.

The earliest reference to equipping the cathedral was in the late twelfth century when Bishop Jocelin decreed that the books and vestments of canons who died intestate should go to the cathedral. Despite other gifts, in 1401 Bishop Matthew de Glendinning deplored the lack of ornaments. The consequence of Bishop Glendinning's concern was the arrangement that anyone appointed to a prebend in the cathedral should pay a part of the revenue from his prebend towards providing ornaments and vestments.

An inventory of the cathedral's possessions in 1432 suggests that by this time it was well provided for. It also shows that the cathedral had acquired not only vestments and vessels but a collection of relics, many of which, such as parts of the True Cross and hairs of the Blessed Virgin, might today be regarded with scepticism. Two relics of St Thomas Becket, however, seem more likely to be authentic. There were some fifty books for liturgical use, some of them chained so that they could not be taken away. These would undoubtedly have included the *Life* of Glasgow's patron saint. There was also the shrine of St Kentigern, ornamented with precious stones, to attract pilgrims. However, from the mid-1470s known benefactors to the cathedral were almost exclusively clerics.

The Glasgow diocese

GLASGOW'S HUGE DIOCESE STRETCHED from the northern end of Loch Lomond to the English border and the Solway, and from the Ayrshire coast to the western boundary of the diocese of St Andrews in Lothian and the

ABOVE
Medieval High Street c. 1520 (detail). Watercolour by David Simon, 2006.

ABOVE
Prayer book of Robert Blacader, owner of the book at prayer before Christ on the Cross, late 15th century

Border country. In the 1260s Glasgow's bishop, John de Cheam, claimed that his diocese should stretch as far south as the Rere Cross at Stainmore, despite the fact that a diocese of Carlisle had been established in 1133.

In 1238 a second archdeaconry was created to help in administering this very large area: the archdeacon of Glasgow for the northern part of the diocese and the archdeacon of Teviotdale for the south. In addition, from the late twelfth century there were deans of Christianity (numbers varying from time to time), assisting both the bishop and the archdeacon in subdivisions of the archdeaconries. By 1300 there were over two hundred parishes. David I founded numerous monasteries of which two of the most important were included in the Glasgow diocese: Jedburgh, where Bishop John was buried in 1147 and Melrose, where Bishop Jocelin died and was buried in 1199.

By 1300, the Glasgow diocese had six major and three lesser houses of male religious orders and one house of nuns (refounded as a collegiate church in the late fourteenth century). By the beginning of the sixteenth century there were seven houses of friars, two in the city itself, those of the Dominicans and the Observant Franciscans on the High Street. By the end of the middle ages there were nearly forty hospitals (a term which covered a variety of pious purposes: sheltering pilgrims, or caring for the sick, the aged and in some cases specifically for lepers).

Three of the hospitals were in Glasgow itself: St Nicholas for twelve old men, the leper hospital of St Ninian at the south end of Glasgow bridge and a hospital for 'the poor and indigent casually coming thereto' founded under the terms of a bequest by Roland Blacader, the sub-dean. A popular benefaction (the equivalent of private or business sponsorship today) of the later middle ages was the collegiate church. Much less expensive to endow than a monastery, these were staffed by a group of canons whose purpose was to sing the daily services and in many cases to pray for the souls of the founder and his family. The diocese had eleven collegiate churches by 1550, one of them in the town, the collegiate church of St Mary of Loreto and St Anne, staffed by a provost, nine canons and three choristers.

Glasgow in national history

Glasgow is rarely mentioned in Scotland's early national history. The earliest reference to the town's inhabitants dates from 1164, when Bishop Herbert rallied them to defeat an invasion by Somerled, ruler of much of the Western Isles. In 1235, a Glasgow troop attacked an Irish force which had been involved in war in Galloway. Most evidence about Glasgow's role in national affairs comes from the activities of the bishops and archbishops. In 1173, at a meeting of the king's council, Bishop Ingram advised King William I against the invasion of England which was to lead to the king's capture.

The War of Independence provides more information about the city. Glasgow's bishop, Robert Wishart, supported Robert Bruce (the future king's grandfather) in his claim to the throne after the death of Alexander III in 1286. When the future king murdered John Comyn, Bishop Wishart absolved him from the sin. Wishart provided Bruce with a royal banner and with vestments from the cathedral treasury when he was inaugurated as king.

The war brought Edward I, his general Aymer de Valence and later Edward II to Glasgow. Edward I ordered tools and materials in the town. Edward III and Edward Balliol held a council in the city, as did Robert II. There is, however, no evidence that Glasgow suffered war damage. In 1544, the earl of Lennox, leader of the pro-English party after the death of James V, was besieged in Glasgow by the earl of Arran.

There is also no evidence about the possible effects on Glasgow of the plague known as the Black Death. It reached Scotland in 1349, but may have been less severe than in other parts of Western Europe.

Royal visits generally took place when the monarch was on the way to another area. In 1222 Alexander II was forced to abandon an expedition to the Western Isles. It was however reported that he had reached Glasgow safely. In 1328 Robert I stopped in Glasgow en route to Ulster. James I dropped by on his way to Ayr in 1424, and James IV rested in Glasgow while on his way to besiege Duchal and Dumbarton Castles in 1489. James conducted judicial business in the city in 1494 and was also in Glasgow before and after an expedition to the Western Isles in 1495, after which Hugh O'Donnell of Tyrconnel came to Glasgow and made an agreement with him, probably against the English.

Up to the mid-thirteenth century several of Glasgow's bishops owed their promotion to service to the king, especially as chancellor (keeper of the king's seal and one of his principal advisers). They often ceased to hold government office on becoming bishops. By the fifteenth century, however, it was usual for bishops to hold government office, as a member of the king's council, secretary to the king, lord treasurer, keeper of the Great Seal (for government business had become so complex that more than one seal was required) and member of the Court of Lord Auditors. Bishops were also often employed as ambassadors, and were members of parliament.

Bishop Andrew de Durisdeer was councillor to James II, procurator of the king at the court of Pope Nicholas V, a member of the council of regency for the young James III, a frequent attender at parliament, a member of the Court of Lords Auditors and one of the ambassadors who visited Denmark to discuss the marriage of James III to Margaret of Denmark.

Bishop Robert Blacader (the future archbishop) took a leading part in the rebellion which led to the defeat and murder of James III in 1488. His reward was a vote in the Scottish parliament that Glasgow should become an archbishopric. As Glasgow's first archbishop Blacader acted as ambassador to Spain and conducted the marriage service of James IV and Margaret Tudor. Archbishop James Beaton crowned James V. Even after 1560, his namesake, the exiled Archbishop Beaton, performed diplomatic services for Mary I and James VI.

Glasgow and the papacy

The clergy were much aware of their connection with the papacy. Prelates were often called upon to act as papal judges delegate that is, to hear a complaint that had been brought to the pope and either to report back or to make a judgment in the case. Bishops attended papal general councils: three, including Walter de St Albans of Glasgow (1208-1232), were present at the Fourth Lateran Council in 1215.

In the thirteenth century popes began to seek positions in Glasgow for Italians as a method of providing income for the growing papal civil service. Pope Gregory IX asked for a prebend in the cathedral for Peter de Curia; in 1247 Gerard of Rome was canon of Renfrew. These papal placemen were presumably two of the four Italian canons mentioned in a document dated

LEFT
Carved stone head, Melrose Abbey

BELOW
Bronze mortars found during excavations at Glasgow Cathedral

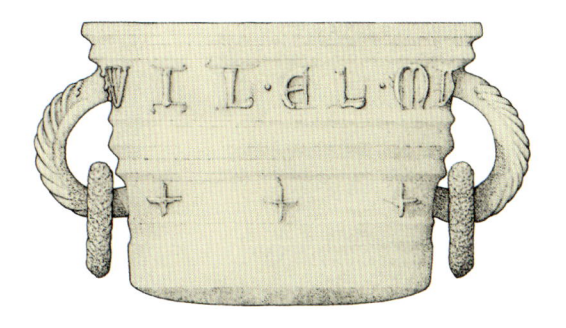

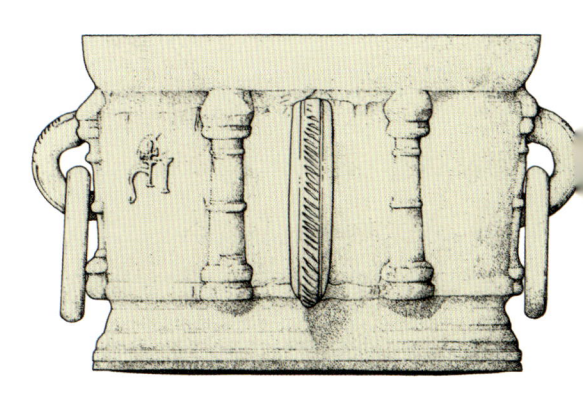

OPPOSITE
Belgian tapestry depicting a banquet in the open air c. 1510

BELOW
Dumbarton Rock, painted glass, Glasgow, 19th century

1248. In the early fourteenth century the dean of Glasgow Cathedral was a member of the famous Florentine banking family of Bardi.

By the fifteenth century the Church in Rome was regarded by many as a job market. This was largely the result of the papacy's claim in 1335 to appoint to every post in the Western Church. A series of supplications to the pope were received in Rome from fifteenth century Scotland. In 1428 John Methven, priest of Lunan in Forfarshire, supplicated the pope to appoint him to the canonry of Ashkirk in Glasgow Cathedral, which was about to become vacant. Glasgow provided the first Scottish cardinal, Bishop Walter de Wardlaw (1383), though he was appointed by an anti-pope, Clement VII of Avignon. When Bishop William Turnbull wanted to set up a university in the city, he had to secure a bull of foundation from Pope Nicholas V which was granted in 1451.

Glasgow's rivals

AN EARLY RIVAL TO GLASGOW'S CLAIM to be the most important place of pilgrimage in central Scotland was nearby Govan. This rapidly developing township may have come to prominence after the sack of the fort on Dumbarton Rock in 870. Govan certainly had an important church set in a distinctive enclosure with relics of St Constantine. Nearby was a related doomster hill, a sixteen foot (five metre) high mound which may have been the focus of court proceedings or ceremonial gatherings. There was also a connection across the river to Partick, a royal possession.

Govan's remarkable collection of carved stones shows that it was a place of major importance in the tenth and eleventh centuries. Perhaps it was the seat of the bishop of Cumbria; if so, however, the establishment of a cathedral at Glasgow put an end to that. When David I granted rights over Govan to Glasgow Cathedral, its status was greatly diminished and it was simply referred to as 'the church of Govan'.

Rutherglen was another nearby centre with which Glasgow had a centuries-long rivalry. It seems to have been given burghal status by David I. As a legal entity, therefore, it was older than Glasgow. William I granted Glasgow Cathedral forty shillings from his revenues from Rutherglen. Alexander II rejected Rutherglen's claim to levy tolls on merchants in Glasgow. In 1304 Bishop Robert Wishart countered this historic impudence with a claim that his officials had an immemorial right to levy tolls on the burgesses of Rutherglen for all goods traded in Glasgow. Although Rutherglen had a market and a fair, Glasgow's position, farther along the Clyde, seems to have blocked its economic expansion. In 1450 James II forbade Rutherglen from interfering with the trading privileges of Glasgow. That restriction was repeated in a judicial decision of 1542.

Renfrew to the south and west was certainly founded by David I, and so was older than Glasgow. It was granted to Walter, son of Alan, ancestor of the Stewarts, but, on the accession of the first Stewart king, Robert II, it again came directly under royal authority. The church was granted to Glasgow Cathedral by David I before 1147 and became a prebend. In 1450 James II forbade the bailies and burgesses of Renfrew from interfering with the privileges of Glasgow. In 1542 a legal decision ordered Renfrew to allow the bringing of goods to Glasgow's market.

Further west, the Royal Burgh of Dumbarton was founded by Alexander II in 1222, but he conceded that burgesses of Glasgow could trade with Argyll and Lennox and the whole kingdom without being hindered by the king's bailies of Dumbarton. In 1275 Alexander III ordered the men of Dumbarton not to trouble the men of Glasgow, since the Glaswegians had had the privilege of trading with Argyll before Dumbarton was founded. A judicial decision of 1469 (ratified by James III) found that the burgh had wronged the community of Glasgow by stopping the latter from buying wine from a French ship on the Clyde.

Glasgow's success against rival burghs is surprising, given that two were earlier foundations and three were royal burghs. The explanation lies certainly in royal support and probably in respect for St Kentigern and the authority his standing gave to Glasgow's bishops and archbishops. Of course, Glasgow's steadily increasing status might also have been in recognition of the tenacity and the trading and craft skills of the town's medieval citizens.

29

power to punish by 'life or

limb'

Law, Courts and People

DAVID SELLAR

An older legal order

THIS CHAPTER COVERS THE PERIOD from the emergence of Scots law as a distinct system in the thirteenth century until the Protestant Reformation of 1560. However a few surviving documents offer tantalising glimpses of an older social and political order. In the early twelfth century, the memory of an independent kingdom of Strathclyde remained sufficiently strong for Earl David, later to be king, to style himself 'Prince of Cumbria' in his famous 'inquest' into the possessions of the diocese of Glasgow. The presence of two 'Judges of Cumbria', Leysyng and Oggo, among those who swore to the possessions, points to the survival of a legal order about which little is known.

As late as the reign of David's grandson Malcolm IV (1153-65) royal charters occasionally address his British subjects in Strathclyde specifically as *Walensibus* (Welsh or Britons) as distinct from the usual French, English and Scots.

The King's law

BY THE END OF THE THIRTEENTH century, however, the king of Scots no longer addressed his subjects by separate nationalities. The 'common law' of Scotland, the law common to all the king's subjects and declared in his courts, was beginning to take shape and the pattern of courts was well established. The king's courts were particularly concerned with issues relating to land and succession to land and also with criminal justice.

The Crown's principal legal and administrative officer at local level was the sheriff. Glasgow lay within the Sheriffdom of Lanark, an important early royal centre. Indeed, until as late as 1975, Glasgow Sheriff Court remained 'The Sheriff Court of Lanark at Glasgow'!

Two of the best known sheriffs of Lanark were both appointed by Edward I. The first was William Heselrig, in later tradition blamed for the killing of the wife and children of William Wallace. The story is that Heselrig was later killed by Wallace in revenge. Certainly it is the case that the 'murder' of the sheriff of Lanark was one of the charges laid against Wallace at his trial in London in 1305.

The second famous sheriff of Lanark, perhaps surprisingly, was Robert Bruce himself, soon to be king, who was appointed sheriff of Lanark and Ayr in 1303. This was at a time when he was temporarily in King Edward's allegiance.

The sheriff court had a wide civil and criminal jurisdiction as, indeed, it still has today. Typically a civil action would commence with a writ or 'brieve' issued by the royal chancery. The issue of a writ required the sheriff to call together an 'inquest' or jury of the leading men of the countryside to decide, for example, a question of succession to land. Or the action might be a simple possessory one concerning goods or money.

On the criminal side, the sheriff would sit with an inquest or 'assize', the forerunner of the criminal jury, with power to punish by 'life or limb', that is, to mutilate or put to death in appropriate cases. Typical crimes, meriting such punishment might be that of a killer caught red-handed, or a thief caught 'infangtheif' ('with the fang'), that is caught red-handed with the stolen goods. Thus Thomas Wood was 'inditit and accusit' in the sheriff court of Fife in 1521 'for the thyftwis steling fra Allane Ramsay of ane hors … quhilk hors was tayntyt (taken) reydhand wyth the said Thomas'[1]. Sentence was duly pronounced that 'the said Thomas sould be haid bundyne to the gallos & hangyt tharone quhil (until) that he wer deyd upone the quhilk (which) dome (sentence) wes gevine'[2].

The most serious offences were known as 'the pleas of the Crown'. Traditionally four in number – murder, rape, robbery and arson – these crimes were reserved to the Crown. The king's justiciar or his deputes would travel the country on regular circuits or 'ayres' seeking out and punishing serious crime, as their successors, the judges of the High Court of Justiciary, do to this day.

A frequent cause of action in the sheriff court was the quasi-criminal offence of 'spuilzie' (spoliation), in which the pursuer claimed that he (or she) had been unlawfully dispossessed of moveable goods. Spuilzie could cover a wide range of goods, animate and inanimate, ranging from cows and sheep to plough-goods or kettles. The penalty was an 'amercement' or fine.

Actions for 'lawburrows' were also common. In lawburrows one party would claim that he had cause to fear bodily harm from another. The threatened claimant would seek to have the accused compelled to find a surety ('borgh' or burrow) that he would not be harmed. The time-honoured phrase was that he should be 'harmless and skaithless'. Thus in the sheriff court of Fife in 1517, Charles Denniston found Adam Lindsay 'souerte & lawborcht to the schiref that Johne Hutoune suld be harmeles and scaithles of hyme'[3]. Actions for lawburrows have continued to be heard by Scottish courts down the centuries. One was raised in Glasgow Sheriff Court as late as 1975, and another in Dumfries Sheriff Court in 2007!

Barony courts

ALSO OPERATING AT LOCAL LEVEL were the courts of powerful lords, courts of barony and of regality, to whom a measure of royal jurisdiction had been delegated. By the end of the middle ages there were hundreds of barony courts in Scotland, exercising powers comparable to the royal sheriff. The enumeration of these powers in charter form made a satisfying jingle (with *sake and soke* and *thol and theme* and *infangandthefe*). Such a listing is held up to gentle ridicule by Sir Walter Scott in his description of the Baron of Bradwardine in *Waverley*.

A more sobering account of the reality of barony jurisdiction in the sixteenth century occurs in a treatise compiled in 1560 for the benefit of the French advisers of Mary of Guise, mother of Mary, Queen of Scots. This sets

ABOVE
William Wallace, Robert Bruce, painted glass, Glasgow, 19th century

1, 2, 3 W C Dickinson (ed.), *The Sheriff Court Book of Fife* (Edinburgh, 1928)

out some of the salient features of the Scottish legal system. After noting that barons "who hold their lands in barony"[4] had power to punish all those who struck or wounded anyone to the effusion of blood, the Discours continues that barons had the same powers to punish thieves and resetters as had sheriffs "and in order to carry out this they have authority to erect within their jurisdiction as many gallows as they please"[5].

Lords of regality were granted even greater powers, sometimes even including the four pleas of the Crown. These grants of barony and regality were not confined to laymen, but could also be granted to the Church. Thus the bishop of Glasgow, in his capacity as a secular lord, had a barony jurisdiction from the twelfth century which was later elevated to regality status by royal charter in 1450.

A much prized right upheld by the barony court of Glasgow was the custom of 'St Mungo's widow'. This gave the widows of those who had held a lease for life in the barony the right to extend the lease for the term of their own lives.

An important privilege of regality was the right to reclaim men or women of the regality who stood accused before other courts. This might even extend to accusations of homicide or 'slaughter' before the royal justiciar. In 1555 a churchman, Mark Ker, abbot of Newbattle, was accused before the Justice-Court along with his brother-in-law John Home, laird of Cowdenknowes, of the wounding and slaughter of some French soldiers in Newbattle itself.

Ker pleaded that 'as he wes ane Kirkman'[6] he should be repledged 'to his Juge Ordinare'[7]. Both Glasgow and St Andrews claimed him as their own. 'Maister James Balfour', well known to later Scottish law students as the author of *Balfours Practicks*, appeared for the archbishop of St Andrews 'as Ordinare to the said Maister Mark (and) desyrit him to be replegit'. William Bannatyne argued that Ker should be repledged to the jurisdiction of the archbishop of Glasgow.

In the event, Mark Ker was repledged to St Andrews. There is no record of any further proceedings against him but if there were, he survived relatively unscathed. After the Reformation Ker turned Protestant, secularised the lands of Newbattle and married. His son, also Mark Ker, Lord Newbattle, was created first earl of Lothian in 1606.

The law of the church

The king's law was not the only law in Scotland. As elsewhere in Western Europe, there was a parallel system of justice which looked to Rome and the pope rather than to any secular ruler. Ecclesiastical courts administered canon law, the universal law of Western Christendom. They operated at two levels.

At diocesan level there was the court of the bishop's 'official', a qualified lawyer with delegated authority from the bishop to act as judge. The court of the official sat on a regular basis and was one of the busiest courts in Scotland.

At a higher level, courts of 'judges-delegate', directly appointed by the pope, might sit on an *ad hoc* basis to resolve a particular dispute. These judges-delegate, generally three in number, were leading churchmen, appointed from the area in question.

The courts of the church exercised remarkably wide powers covering many aspects of daily life which would now be the concern of secular courts. They would deal, for example, with all questions concerning the validity of marriage.

Marriages were frequently challenged on the grounds that the parties stood in the forbidden degrees of relationship. If they were related to each other up to and including the fourth degree, that is if they had a great-great grandparent in common, they could not lawfully marry. Or a prohibition might arise from an earlier marriage if a second spouse was too closely related to the first. Even intercourse outwith marriage with a relative of a prospective spouse many years before might be enough to invalidate a marriage.

The church courts also had jurisdiction over questions of legitimacy, over wills and executry, over agreements supported by an oath, and in cases of scandal caused by offensive words or deeds. On all such matters the secular courts would defer to the decisions of the church courts. In modern terms, much of the law of husband and wife, parent and child, succession, contract and defamation lay within the jurisdiction of the ecclesiastical courts.

One of the best recorded disputes in medieval Scotland was heard in 1233 at Irvine and at Ayr by a court of judges-delegate appointed by the pope, comprising Lawrence, dean of Carrick, Richard, dean of Cunningham and the master of the schools of Ayr. The case concerned the ownership of a piece of land named Monachkeneran, which was situated to the north of the river Clyde near Old Kilpatrick, very close to the northern end of the present Erskine Bridge.

Monachkeneran was only one of a number of estates lying between the Clyde and the Kilpatrick hills which were in dispute. It was alleged that these estates rightfully belonged to the church of Old Kilpatrick, itself now attached to the abbey of Paisley, but that they had been deliberately granted to laymen by Dugald, the rector of Kilpatrick. Accordingly the Abbey of Paisley, whose register preserves an account of the case, sued Gilbert, son of Samuel of Renfrew, who claimed to be the current owner of Monachkeneran, before the judges-delegate. The interest of the case lies not only in its description of the legal process, but also in the vivid picture of medieval life which emerges from the witness statements.

Many of the witnesses had been familiar with the parish of Kilpatrick all their lives. They all agreed that the land did belong to the church and its ownership had been wilfully alienated by Dugald, the rector.

The first witness at Irvine was Alexander Fitzhugh who swore that he could remember a man named Bede Ferdan living in a big house made of

BELOW LEFT
Seal of Bishop Walter (1208-32)

4, 5 Peter G B McNeill (ed.), *Discours Particulier D'Escosse* in David Sellar (ed.), *Miscellany II* (Edinburgh, 1984) 6, 7 *Pitcairn's Criminal Trials* (Edinburgh, 1833)

ABOVE

Decree from the Court of Session Edinburgh, 4 June 1575, permitting Glasgow to extract 'a ladleful of every sack of victual' coming to the Glasgow market via Rutherglen.

wattles to the east of the church of Kilpatrick sixty years earlier. Bede had held the land of Monachkeneran in the name of the church in return for receiving and entertaining strangers. Fitzhugh said that when he was a boy he and his father had sometimes gone there as guests.

The next witness was Thomas Gaskel. He also remembered Bede Ferdan and said that Bede's son Cristin had held the land after him on the same terms. He was able to detail the estates owned by the church, including Cochmanach and Edinbernan – still recognisable today as Cochno and Edinbarnet. Dugald, the rector, next gave evidence and confessed that he had indeed wrongfully alienated the titles of Monachkeneran and many other estates which belonged to the church because he did not wish to offend his father and his brother, the powerful earls of Lennox.

At a later hearing, in Ayr, Malcolm Beg appeared as a witness and swore that he too had seen Bede keeping his house beside the graveyard of the church, adding that he, the witness, had held the estate of Kathconnen for the church, but had alienated it out of fear. Other witnesses spoke to the same effect. Gilbethoc added the significant information that the memorable Bede had been killed while defending the rights and liberty of the church.

Gilbert, the defender, chose not to put in an appearance. Unsurprisingly the judges-delegate found that the lands rightfully belonged to the church, and held Gilbert liable in expenses for thirty pounds, a truly enormous sum. They called on the bishop of Glasgow to execute their judgement. Despite this ruling the dispute rumbled on for another sixty years.

The most distinguished official of medieval Glasgow was William Elphinstone who held the post from 1471 to 1478. Elphinstone was born in Glasgow and an early graduate of the university. He became chancellor of Scotland and bishop of Aberdeen where he is still revered as the founder of Aberdeen University.

Thanks to the diligence of Elphinstone's biographer, Leslie Macfarlane, something is known of Elphinstone's work as official of Glasgow. Macfarlane notes a marriage dispute which came before Elphinstone in 1471. Walter Turnbull of Gargunnnock and his wife Margaret Norvele had been married with children for many years. Margaret, however, claimed that the marriage was invalid as she and Walter were related within the prohibited degrees.

Walter claimed that a dispensation had been granted allowing him and Margaret to marry, despite their being in the prohibited degrees. He requested William Elphinstone, as official of Glasgow, to make a formal record of the depositions of witnesses regarding the granting of the dispensation.

The story revealed by the witnesses, although unremarkable at the time, appears quite peculiar to modern readers. It involves King James II, James Kennedy, bishop of St Andrews and William Turnbull, bishop of Glasgow and founder of Glasgow University.

About seventeen years previously James II, described as 'last deceased at Roxburgh'[8] (where he had been killed by an exploding cannon), had given 'one of the ladies of Gargunnock'[9], Margaret Norvele, to Bishop Turnbull in marriage for one of his kinsmen. Turnbull duly nominated his nephew Walter as the lady's husband. In making such a gift of marriage the king was exercising a common feudal right. Most marriages in the upper echelons of medieval society were arranged. However, the consent of both parties to the marriage, freely given, remained essential in canon law.

As Walter and Margaret were related in the forbidden degrees a dispensation to marry had been sought. The bishop of St Andrews had granted the necessary dispensation under license from the Pope. One witness added the further detail that the bishop of St Andrews had wanted twenty nobles (English gold coins each worth one third of a pound) for granting the dispensation, but the bishop of Glasgow had refused to give more than ten merks (rather less in Scots money). The whole proceeding was recorded on 6 April 1471, 'dated and done in the consistorial place of Glasgow Cathedral'[10], that is, the north-west aisle, the regular meeting place of the official's court.

In 1510, the protocol book of Cuthbert Simon, chapter clerk of Glasgow, records a scandal in the official's court in which the Scots words leap out from the surrounding Latin. Andrew Birkmyre, a vicar of the choir of Glasgow, confessed before the archbishop and the cathedral chapter that he had had the effrontery to declare in the official's court, that the official, Martin Rede, was biased and that he had no power to fasten him and bind his feet.

One witness in the case recollected that the actual words spoken by Birkmyre were, 'It sall pass your power to fessyn my feyt; ye ar partial; ye dow nocht to fessyn a scheip hede'[11]. A second witness testified that Birkmyre had added, 'I sett nocht by you a fert of your ers'![12] Birkmyre was called on to acknowledge these contemptuous words and was obliged to ask pardon of the archbishop and the official in court on his bended knees.

Burgh and burgh court

THE MOST IMPORTANT COURT in the daily lives of the citizens of Glasgow was the burgh court. Burghs were divided into royal burghs, burghs of barony and burghs of regality. Glasgow was an ecclesiastical burgh of barony, later of regality, as too were Paisley and St Andrews. Rutherglen, by contrast, was a royal burgh from as early as the reign of David I (1124-53) with extensive trading privileges which gave rise to regular disputes with the bishop's burgh of Glasgow. Although increasingly powerful and wealthy, Glasgow remained

8, 9, 10 Leslie J Macfarlane, *William Elphinstone and the Kingdom of Scotland 1431-1514* (Aberdeen, 1985) 11, 12 J Bain and C Rogers (eds), *The Protocol Book of Cuthbert Simon 1499-1513* (Grampian Club, 1875)

an ecclesiastical burgh until 1636, when it was at last elevated to the status of a royal burgh.

The burgh, like the barony, had its own court. In Glasgow the court sat first, it would seem, in the open air, on the site of the 'Muthill' or 'Maitland' croft, to the south of the later Trongate. In the fifteenth century the court was presided over by the provost and bailies. The most important courts or 'head courts' were held three times a year: at Michaelmas (early in October); at Yule; and at 'Pasche' (Easter), this last being held later at Whitsunday.

The Michaelmas and Yule head courts were held in the Tolbooth and the Whitsunday court at 'the Symmerhill', near the corner of the present day West Graham and Cambridge Streets. Less important sittings of the burgh court were held on a fortnightly basis. All burgesses were bound to attend the head courts as a matter of duty and the lesser courts if specifically summoned. The officers of court included the 'doomster', (whence the surname 'Dempster') whose function it was to pronounce the sentence or 'doom' of the court.

Like the baron court, the sheriff court and the king's court of justiciary, the burgh court was 'fenced' to indicate the start of formal proceedings. Originally, when courts met in the open air, the ceremony of 'fencing' was undertaken quite literally. Later, however, a set form of words would indicate that the court had been duly fenced:

"I defend, and biddis, in our liege Lord the king's behalfe of Scotland, and in the behalfe of the Lord that this Court aucht, and his Baillie, that here is, that na man distrouble this Court unlawfullie under the paine that may follow; or make him to speik for any, but (without) leave asked and obtained".[13]

The formula of fencing gradually fell into disuse in most of Scotland's courts, although it continued in Glasgow Sheriff Court within living memory.

An important function of the Whitsunday head court was to supervise the riding of the marches. These 'common ridings', processing round the bounds of the burgh, were occasions for ceremony, civic pride and general rejoicing, as still remains the case in the Borders. Judging from later accounts, the burgh magistrates of Glasgow, accompanied by 'outlandimers' (surveyors), burgesses and the 'honest men of the town', processed around the bounds, preceded by the town's banner or 'palyeoun' and by drummers. Afterwards there was a civic feast.

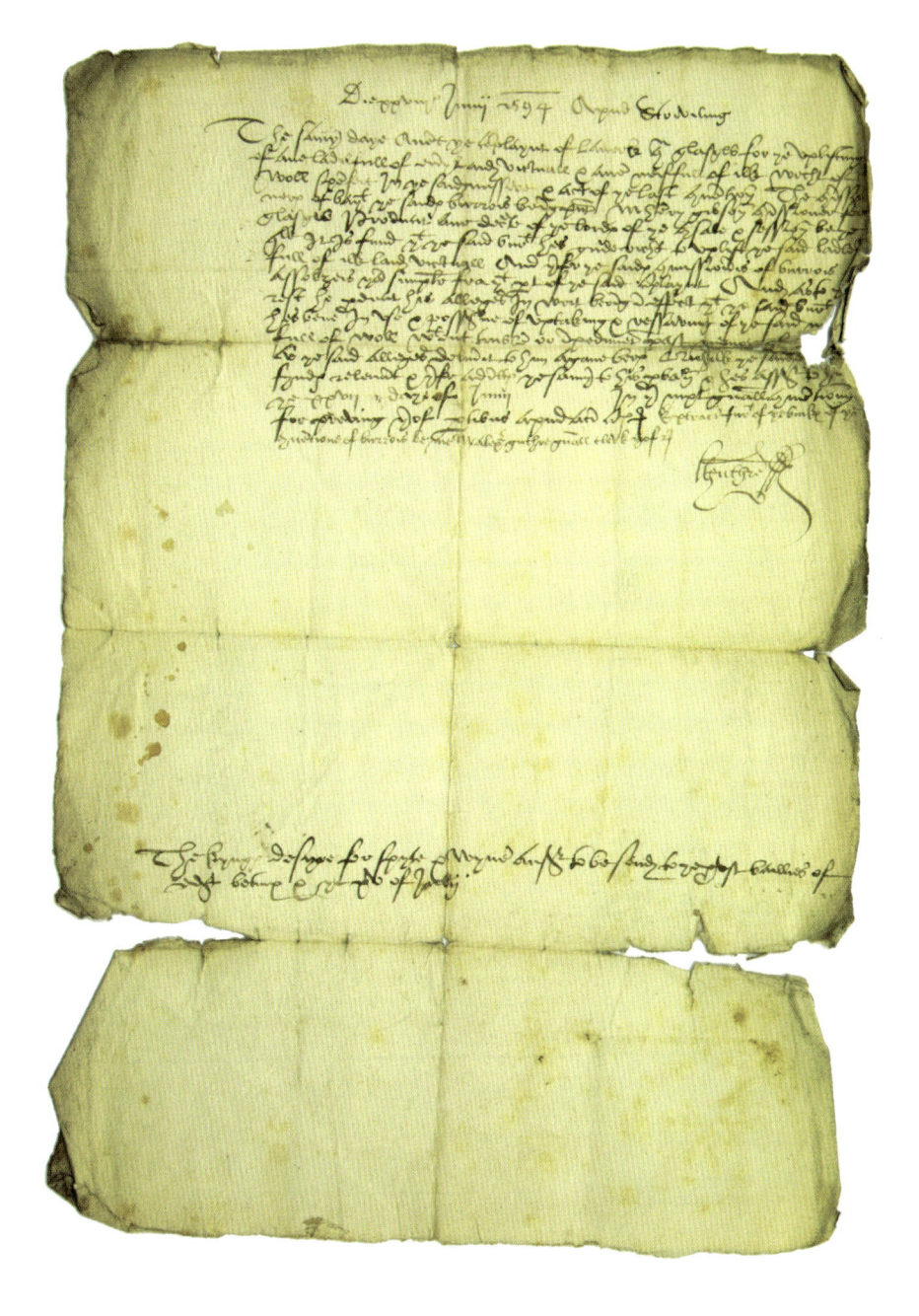

Acts of Parliament were proclaimed at head courts, not least those commanding the holding of 'wapinschaws', or armed musters, for the defence of the realm. In 1424, it was ordained that "in ilk sherifdome of the realme there be maid wapynschawingis four tymis in the yere."[14] The following year it was specified:

"That al burgessis and induellaris within the burrowis of the realme in lik maner be anarmyt (armed) & harnest & mak wapinschawing within the burowis of the realme in lik manere foure tymis in the yere."[15]

By an act of 1429 burgesses were required to attend these musters equipped for war with hat and doublet, coat of mail, sword and buckler, bow and knife: "and at (that) he that is na bow-man haf a gude ax or wapynis of fens (defence)."[16] An act of 1491, following the earlier acts, repeated the provisions for the holding of wapinshaws, going on to condemn 'unprofitable sports' such as football and golf, "In na place of the Realme, be usit fut bawis, gouff or uthir sic unprofitable sportis."[17] Instead, burgesses were expected to

ABOVE
Act of Court, Stirling, 1594, supporting Glasgow's right to extract 'a ladleful of each load of victual' arriving in Glasgow via Lanark.

LEFT
Medieval street football. Football was condemned as an 'unprofitable sport' in an Act of 1491.

13 W C Dickinson (ed.), *The Barony Court Book of Carnwath, 1523-1542* (Edinburgh, 1937) 14, 15, 16, 17 T Thomson and Cosmo Innes (eds), *Acts of the Parliaments of Scotland* (Edinburgh 1814-75)

attend at the butts for archery practice for the "commoun gude & defence of the realme."[18]

Some other acts have a quite contemporary ring. In 1436 an act was passed setting closing time in pubs,

"The King and the tre estates has ordanyt that na man in burghe be fundyn in tavernys at wyne, aile or beir efter the straik of ix houres and the bell that salbe rongyn in the said burghe. The quhilkis beande fundyn (that is, anyone found in taverns after nine o'clock) the aldermen and bailzeis sal put thame in the kingis presone (prison). The quhilk gif (if) thai do not thai sall pay for ilk tyme at (that) thai be fundyn culpabill befor the chawmerlane (the chamberlain) fifty shillings."[19]

The burgh court could also pass its own statutes or regulations. For example, it was "statute and ordanit" in 1581, "That na hydis, skynnis, ischewis (offal), nor na other filthie thingis be waschin in the burne of Molyndoner."[20] Despite this and later similar regulations, by the eighteenth century the Molendinar burn has been likened to a common cesspool, serving the greater part of Glasgow.

The burgh court's jurisdiction was comparable to that of the barony and the sheriff court in both civil and criminal matters. Burgh law too, was the king's law, although there were some laws and customs peculiar to burghs. Thus in the early period, while serfdom was still permitted, a man who remained in a burgh unchallenged for a year and a day was recognised as a free man. Also burgesses were excused trial by battle while this still remained a recognised method of dispute-settlement in other courts. In 1216 Pope Innocent III addressed a papal bull to the faithful in the kingdom of Scotland, as he did to others in Christendom, condemning trial by battle (duellum) as a 'pestiferous custom'.

Few records survive of proceedings in the medieval Glasgow burgh court. One exception is the record of an inquest held in the head court of the burgh at Michaelmas 1325 which found that Thomas de Aula was entitled, by right of his wife Cristian, to succeed to lands in the burgh which had belonged to Cristian's father Nicholas Tigrim.

A very different type of case was decided by a burgh head court in 1574 when three men and a woman were, 'Dilatit as leper, and ordaneit to be viseit (visited) and gif thai be fund sa (and if they were found so), to be secludit of the toun to the hospital at the Brigend'[21]; that is, at the leper hospital at the south end of the bridge from Glasgow to the Gorbals.

A full record survives of a curious case heard in four successive Glasgow head courts in 1478 and 1479 concerning land in 'Ratenraw' (Rottenrow). An annual payment was due to the vicars of the choir of Glasgow from the land. Unfortunately it had not been paid for many years. The land was said to be, 'Destitute of al bigging (building) and reparacion in all parts … the grounde remanande wast and unhabit (waste and uninhabited)'[22].

Through their procurator, or spokesman, the vicars claimed that, as a consequence of continued non-payment, they were entitled to the ownership of the ground. The serjeant of court was sent to inspect the property and report back. He found it to be 'wast and unhabit and not strenzeable'[23], that is, not worth poinding for the annual payment.

The vicars of the choir repeated their claim at the next two sittings of the court. At a fourth court held in the tolbooth on 26th January 1479, Alexander Heriot, as procurator for the vicars, reported that, after the third sitting of the court, a proclamation had been made at the market cross calling on the debtor or his representatives to pay within forty days, according to burgh law, or forfeit the land. As no payment had been made, he asked the court for 'ward and doom' of the land in default of payment.

The court being 'ryply and weil avisit'[24] on the issues affecting the Rottenrow land, John Michelson, the burgh clerk, was commanded to instruct John Neilson, dempster of court, to pronounce the sentence (or doom) of the court, that the vicars of the choir had made out their case and had lawfully won and obtained the land in default of payment. The procurator, Alexander Heriot, then asked that a formal record or 'instrument' of the case be made, thus saving the details for posterity.

On the criminal side, although the burgh court had power over life and limb, sentence of death to hang on the city's gallows appears to have been relatively rare. Some evidence suggests that Glasgow's first gallows were located at Townhead but latterly, as the name suggests, they were set at the end of Gallowgate. Death sentences were passed more often for theft than for homicide.

Actions for assault, especially 'bloodwite', were far more common, resulting in a financial penalty. Bloodwite arose when there was an accusation of assault that had left the victim, in the words of the old laws, 'blaa and blody'. Even bruising could give rise to an action for bloodwite. If found guilty the offender was liable to pay a 'wite' or fine to the court, with the possibility of a further fine to the injured party for any harm or 'skaith' sustained if he or she – for women as well as men might be involved in actions for bloodwite – was judged blameless in the matter.

Other punishments meted out by the burgh court included banishment from the burgh, being put in the stocks or pillory (the 'juggs'), whipping, branding, or being nailed by the ear to the tron. In Stirling, the punishment of 'creeling' was used. Offenders were put in a 'creel' which was suspended from a beam near the top of the tolbooth at the pleasure of the provost and bailies. In Ayr, 'common sklanderers' might be suspended in a cage for three hours.

Summing up

Scotland's medieval courts have been criticised both by contemporaries and by modern historians. Their proceedings were satirised by two of the greatest poets to write in Scots, Robert Henryson and Sir David Lindsay of the Mount. Henryson, writing about 1500, attacked corruption in the courts, clerical and lay, in his *Tale of the Dog, the Sheep and the Wolf*, written in the manner of Aesop's *Fables*. The Dog sues the Sheep before the Wolf as judge in the church court. The Sheep tries to decline the Wolf as a partial judge who, 'Hes bene richt odious to me, for with your tuskis ravenous hes slane full mony kinnismen off mine'.

In the event, the Sheep is literally fleeced, being reduced to selling the very wool off his back. Henryson likens the Wolf to a sheriff,

"This Wolf I likkin to a Schiref stout,
Quhilk byis ane forfalt (forfeit) at the Kingis hand,
And hes with him ane cursit Assyis about,
And dytis (indicts) all the pure man up on land".

A generation later, Sir David Lindsay mocked the language and procedure of the church courts in his famous *Satire of the Three Estates*:

"Thay gave me first a thing thay called *citandum*;
Within aucht days I gat bot *lybellandum*;
Within ane moneth I gat ad *opponendum*;
In half and yeir I gat *interloquendum*;
And syne I gat, how call ye it? – ad *replicandum*;
Bot I could never ane word yit understand him".

Less poetically, Lord President Cooper, a distinguished modern legal historian, described the medieval court structure in Scotland as 'a chaotic welter of overlapping jurisdictions'[25].

These criticisms are unduly harsh. The medieval court system, baron courts perhaps excepted, served Scotland well enough for many centuries. It helped to maintain order and control in Glasgow through to the Reformation and well beyond. Indeed the procedure of the medieval canon law, satirised by Sir David Lindsay, became the model for legal procedure not only in Scotland but in most of western Europe.

ABOVE
Stained glass small rectangular panel with fox preaching to sheep. English, 15th century

22, 23, 24 *Registrum Episcopatus Glasguensis* (Bannatyne and Maitland Clubs, 1843) 25 Lord Cooper of Culross, *The Dark Age of Scottish Legal History, 1350-1650* (Edinburgh and London, 1957)

the influence of the church was all

pervasive

The Role of the Church
DR MARY MCHUGH

The inquest of David

IN MEDIEVAL GLASGOW THE influence of the church, in the form of parish, diocese, religious orders and in its role in burgh, barony and education, was all pervasive. It began with Kentigern.

The legends concerning Glasgow's patron, St Kentigern or Mungo, who probably died around 614 AD, are well-known. However, after his death, the history of the church of Glasgow becomes uncertain. It re-emerges in the lifetime of David, the youngest son of the marriage of King Malcolm III to St Margaret of Scotland. David was King of Scots from 1124 until his death in 1153. Prior to that, he had become Prince of Cumbria and ruler of an extensive territory, stretching from Glasgow to Berwick.

David and his siblings had sought refuge and support from the English monarch after the deaths, within four days in 1093, of their parents and their elder brother, Edward. While associated with the English court, David also met many of the incoming Norman-French families, many of whom like the Fitzalan (later better known as Stewart) and de Brus (Bruce) families, he encouraged to come to Scotland.

David's territories and responsibilities straddled the border between Scotland and England. It was as ruler of this large area that David promoted a survey (or inquest) of the medieval church in Glasgow. David's inquest was encouraged by Glasgow's bishop, John, and recorded between 1114 and 1124. Such surveys were initiated for political or ecclesiastical reasons or, as is most likely in this case, a combination of both.

The inquest was designed to survey the extent of all lands belonging to the church in Glasgow and its surrounding areas. It seems to confirm that Glasgow had always enjoyed religious significance as the site of the hermitage and tomb of St Mungo. The Glasgow diocese may well have held extensive possessions prior to the twelfth century, including the church of Hoddam in Annandale (in present day Dumfries and Galloway). The church at Hoddam seems originally to have been a monasteria or minster and, as with other minsters, probably served a large district through clergy resident at a central church.

The inquest also provides evidence that the bishops of Glasgow, and lay landowners, had founded churches prior to the twelfth century on their episcopal estates, and mentions specifically the churches of Morebattle, Peebles and Traquair. It would be wrong to assume that all churches which are first mentioned in writing in the twelfth century were necessarily new. It is quite possible that, before this date, churches were looked on almost as part of the landscape and went along with any grant of land, unless specifically exempted.

The identification of earlier landholdings in David's survey did not guarantee their preservation. Royal land grants, and increasing Norman influence in the course of the twelfth century, helped to sweep away many ancient boundaries. Bishops found their influence over churches severely tested and disputes arose between lay owners and bishops.

Much land which appears previously to have belonged to the church passed into lay hands during the course of the twelfth century. This is particularly true in the diocese of Glasgow. Lands previously possessed by the bishops of Glasgow within Annandale had been confirmed to Robert de Brus (Bruce) between 1141 and 1152. A charter of Malcolm IV (1153-1165) refers specifically to lands from which the church of Glasgow had drawn rents and which Malcolm and his predecessors had granted to their barons and knights.

Much of the early medieval history of Glasgow, both civic and ecclesiastical, is obscure. Although three individuals, bearing the title bishop of Glasgow, have been identified in the eleventh and early twelfth century, they appear to be associated with the ongoing claims of the archdiocese of York to authority over the church in Scotland. However they may also provide evidence for the continuation of the Christian community in Glasgow in the centuries between Kentigern's death and David's inquest.

The exact relationship between Glasgow and neighbouring Govan at this time is unclear. Govan is not specified in David's inquest. While archaeology has indicated that Govan was an important Christian centre Glasgow's status continued to be enhanced by the belief that this was the site of St Kentigern's church. The awkward site of the twelfth century cathedral was selected as this was believed to be the location of Kentigern's tomb.

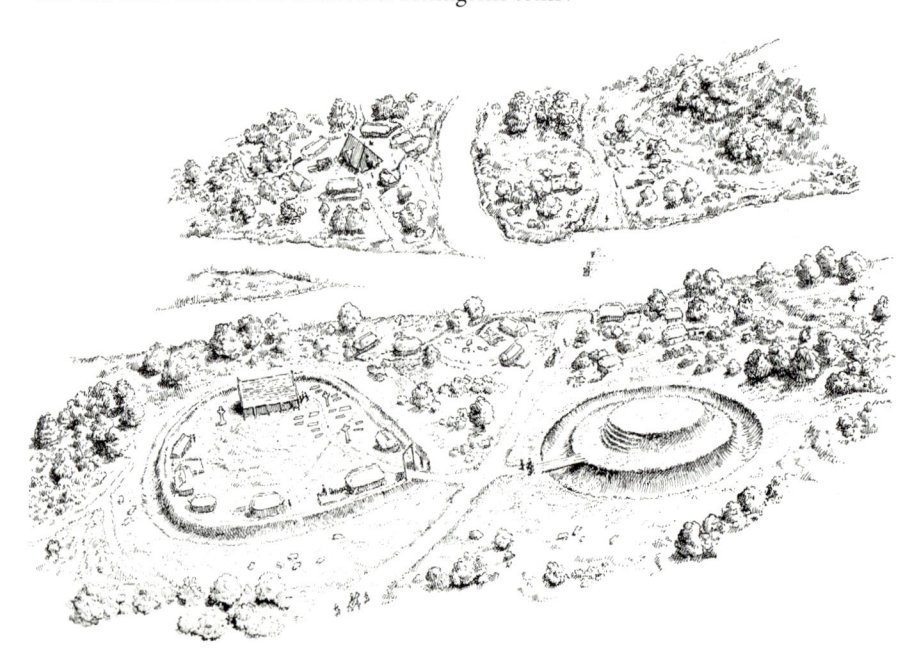

It may be that Glasgow's early claim as Strathclyde's most important religious centre, and therefore to house the kingdom's bishop, was superseded by Govan with its important collection of tenth century Christian carved stones. Govan may well have been superseded in turn by the renewed cult of Kentigern in the twelfth century and by the establishment of Glasgow's cathedral.

The possessions of the church of Glasgow, as recorded in the inquest, included several estates near the burgh, whose development would be important for the growth of the church. Among these were 'Conclud' (possibly an older name for Monkland which extended westwards as far as Kinclaith at Glasgow Green), Ramshorn (near to Rottenrow and Ingram

ABOVE
Facsimile edition of the Life of St. Kentigern now held by the City of Glasgow

BELOW
Sites dedicated to St. Kentigern

RIGHT
View of Govan and Partick c. 1000, reconstruction of Govan Old Parish Church and the Doomster Hill by Chris Brown

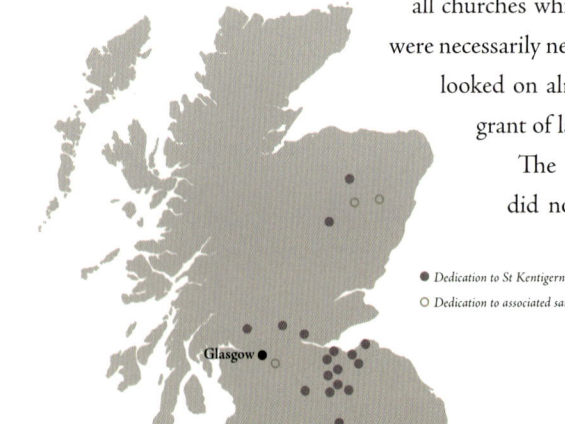

LEFT
Boundaries of the Glasgow diocese, 12th century

BELOW
Govan sarcophagus, mid 9th-mid 10th century, decorated with interlaced ribbons and animals, discovered in 1855 in Govan Old churchyard

Street), Possilpark, Garioch, Partick, Kirklee, lands around Shettleston, and Badermonoc. Barlanark was called 'Pathelanerhc' in the inquest, and was among the oldest possessions of the church in Glasgow.

Grants of estates such as Govan and Partick may have been one form of compensation for the acquisition of Glasgow possessions such as Ballain/Bedlay (the acquisition of which proved to be temporary) by Malcolm IV's brothers, William I (the Lion) and David, Earl of Huntingdon. King David I (1124-1153), with his son Henry, granted the lands of Govan to Glasgow cathedral before 1152, stating, "You are to know that I have given and granted to the church of St Mungo of Glasgu and to the bishopric of the same church Guven, with all its bounds".[26]

Govan (latterly along with the whole of Partick, Shields, Gorbals and Polmadie) was made a prebend of Glasgow Cathedral by Bishop Herbert (1147-64), and encompassed,

"The church of Guvan with all ecclesiastical rights pertaining to the same church, and the islands between Guvan and Perthec and that part of Perthec which King David of Scotland gave as a dower to the church of Glasgu at its dedication, and an [or the] other part of Perthec which the same king David gave to the aforesaid church of Glasgu and to Bishop John and his successors".[27] There appears to be no evidence of any dispute or disagreement over these grants. Glasgow's authority was gradually increasing.

If the, probably spurious, claims of York are ignored, it was also while David was ruler of southern Scotland that the diocese of Glasgow was re-established, with the appointment of Bishop John sometime between 1114 and 1118. The boundaries of the diocese and therefore Glasgow's ecclesiastical jurisdiction were wide. Bishop John's diocese seemingly covered the same ground as David's territories. This was an extensive landscape stretching as far south as the Solway Firth.

The bishop's estate

THE BOUNDARIES OF THE GLASGOW diocese must be distinguished from the bishop's estate. Property was held throughout the diocese, and from these lands (later to be increasingly feued and leased) and their rents, successive bishops generated income. Bishops, as well as religious houses, also appropriated parishes and prebends. The income from some parishes such as Govan was appropriated 'to the bishop's table', which meant that income from Govan was used to support the bishop of Glasgow's household. The bishop was, in turn, expected to dispense charity and to provide hospitality to the poor.

In 1561, Mary, Queen of Scots and her Council instructed a property survey as a means of assessing ecclesiastical wealth. From the rentals listed the, by then archbishop, of Glasgow could count on an income yielding £1,000 in cash and around £2,000 in kind. The following were included as having contributed income in cash or kind;

- the barony of Carstairis (Carstairs) and corn from the mylne (mill),
- the baronies of Ancrum, Lilliesleif, and Askirk,
- the barony and mylne of Stobo,
- the barony of Edlistoun, the Maines of the Lang Coit, Kirkland of Cambusnethan,
- Halfpenny land of Car(r)ick,
- Nudry Foster (probably Niddrie Forest) in Lothian and
- Bishops Forrest in Nidisdaill (Nithsdale).[28]

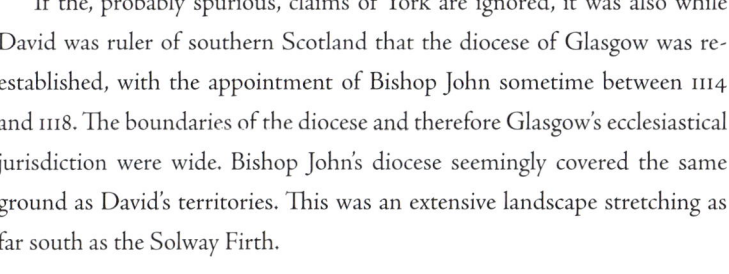

---

26 Ian Cowan, edited by James Kirk, *The Organisation of Secular Cathedral Chapters* in *The Medieval Church in Scotland* (Edinburgh, 1995) 27 Rev Tom A Davidson Kelly, *The Prebend of Govan 1150-1560*, on the Friends of Govan Old website (www.govanold.org.uk) 28 James Kirk (ed.), *Scottish Ecclesiastical Rentals at the Reformation* (Oxford University Press, 1995)

As well as his castle beside the cathedral, the archbishop of Glasgow had a manor house at Lochwood, six miles to the north-east, and other outposts scattered across his archdiocese, such as mills and a further castle at Partick. Partick's extensive grounds were famous for orchards. Lochwood was noted for hunting, and Bishop's Loch for fish.

As a feudal lord the bishop's estate could also have various granges, as may have been the case at Blairtummock. The lands of Barlannerc cum Budlornac were added by Bishop Herbert to the prebend of Cadzow (Hamilton) sometime before 1172. By 1322 Barlanark's status was that of a separate prebend, which, unusually, did not appropriate a parish church, but continued to derive its income from its extensive landholdings. It is claimed that the name Barlanark originates from Bar-lenerk, 'high clearing in the forest'.

The area close to Barlanark was chosen as the country home of the bishops of Glasgow, with their residence at Lochwood. Not far from Lochwood, within the hunting territory of the bishop's forest, Provan Hall (which can still be visited) was built in the fifteenth century. This house is said to have been used as a hunting lodge on visits by King James IV. Barlanark, later known as Provan, was a crown grant, and it may be for this reason that in 1490 King James IV reputedly held the prebend in his role as a canon of the cathedral and 'Lord of Provan'.

The name 'Provan' itself may have been derived from the word 'prebend'. The term 'Lordship of Provan' appears to be a medieval title used from the fourteenth and fifteenth centuries onwards. The prebend of Provan did not have a well-defined territory but came to include Barlanark, Barmulloch, Balornock, added by Bishop Herbert (1147-1167), and the lands of Roder or Riddrie. In 1322, King Robert I (the Bruce) conferred on the then canon, John Wishart, the hunting right known as 'free warren'. The use of the term Lord of Provan became increasingly common in the years which followed.

The bishop's barony

Within the boundaries of the medieval diocese, and covering an area roughly similar to that of the modern city of Glasgow, was the bishop's barony. Medieval bishops were both ecclesiastical superiors and secular lords. Grants of land might be made in free barony, or in free regality. In 1241 a royal charter also granted the bishop the mainly hunting rights of 'free forest'.

The limit of the barony of Glasgow's eastern expansion from 1140 became the lands of Newbattle Abbey at Drumpellier near Coatbridge. By 1242 Garioch, now part of modern Maryhill, appears as a boundary of the bishop's barony on its north-western limit. By the same date there were boundaries also at Possil and Kenmore. By 1164 the lands of Conclud (Monkland) eastwards adjoining the Newbattle lands, were donated to that abbey by Bishop Herbert. However in the late thirteenth century Carmyle and much of Monkland were detached from Newbattle's lands in Monkland and reunited with the bishop's barony under Bishop John de Cheam (1259-1268).

The medieval bishop's barony has been estimated to have contained 18,200 hectares. By the sixteenth century it had been divided into four wards, Govan, Partick, Badermonoc (encompassing all the land from Auchinairn and Robroyston to Gartinqueen) and Shettleston. The medieval barony's principal subjects were the 'rentallers' or farmers who paid rents and dues to the bishop. Tenants were obliged to grind their grain at the barony's mills. Not all the barony land could be cultivated. The Easter and Wester Commons and the Gallowmuir were used for cattle pasturage and to supply fuel.

Administration and power

In both his civil and ecclesiastical spheres, the bishop had officers to help in the management of the diocese and the barony. Archdeacons could discipline both clergy and laity while the dean dealt with moral offences and confirmed testaments valued at less than £40.

By the fifteenth century there were clear signs of a development towards a burgh constitution. The office of provost came into being in the early 1450s. Archbishops Blacader and Dunbar both made their brothers provosts, with the appointment of provosts often being determined largely by political pressure on the archbishops.

By the 1440s Glasgow citizens had some independent rights over the common land and by 1444 they had acquired a town clerk. Although it may have existed earlier the first reference to a town council was in 1501. However other officials, such as the common liners, who carried out divisions of property and settled boundary disputes, existed as early as 1464.

The chamberlain was a cleric and organised the rent collecting. However, one of the oldest offices seems to have been that of bailie, who could be a layman. Bailies presided over the barony and also assisted in collecting the bishop's revenues. The bailies were initially appointed annually by the bishops although, in royal burghs, the burgesses had long been choosing their own bailies, probably since the reign of Robert I (1306-1329). Unlike the provosts, the bailies were always citizens of Glasgow.

Supported by their array of officials and fellow clerics, Glasgow's bishops were involved not only in the ecclesiastical life of the archdiocese but also in

ABOVE
Provan Hall
(built mid 15th century)

RIGHT
Seals of Bishop Jocelin
(1175-99); Robert Wishart
(1272-1316)

29 Geoffrey Barrow, *Robert Bruce* (Edinburgh University Press, 1982)

added to the structure. There is clear evidence that five of Glasgow's bishops were buried in the cathedral although there may be as many as six further, unrecorded, episcopal burials within its walls.

The erection of a cathedral chapter to administer the cathedral followed closely on the restoration of the diocese. Members of the chapter, known as canons, possessed a prebend in the cathedral. Prebends were commonly connected not only to cathedrals but also to collegiate churches. Bishop John appears to have created a chapter of six prebends including those of Glasgow, Renfrew and Hamilton. His work was continued by Bishop Herbert (1147-1164) who established the prebend of Govan.

Initially, the canon prebendaries of Glasgow appear to have been supported by a common fund. However, by the thirteenth century, supporting a prebend by appropriating a parish church had become a virtually universal practice, although Barlanark would remain as a notable exception. Appropriation became a feature of the system which came into existence from the time of David I (1124-1153). An attempt to limit, or at least regulate, this process of annexing parishes is seen in the statement of Pope Lucius III to Jocelin, bishop of Glasgow which declared, "It is unlawful for the religious, dwelling in your diocese to hold any parish church in their hand when it falls vacant or to institute perpetual vicars in any such without your consent".[30]

The original limits of the parish of Glasgow appear to have been confined to the town itself and several adjacent properties including Shettleston, to which Barlanark was added at a later date. A parish therefore existed before the community became a burgh sometime between 1175-1178. King William the Lion also granted to Bishop Jocelin the right to hold a weekly Thursday market and all the liberties of a king's burgh. A few years later, probably between 1189 and 1198, King William authorised Bishop Jocelin and his

LEFT
Glasgow Cathedral towers, drawing by W L Leitch, mid 19th century

BELOW
The Shrine of St Kentigern, lower church, Glasgow Cathedral

public affairs. Over the centuries a number of them achieved notably high civil office. Bishop William de Bondington (1233-1258) served as chancellor of Scotland. Of Bishop Robert Wishart (1271-1316) it is stated that he was,

"One of the great figures in the struggle for Scottish independence, the statesman of the period 1286 to 1291, the patron and friend of Wallace and Bruce, the persistent opponent of Plantagenet pretensions, an unheroic hero of the long war".[29]

Bishop John Cameron (1426-1446) served as secretary to King James I, and was made chancellor in 1427.

The cathedral and chapter

THE TERM CATHEDRAL IS from the Latin *cathedra*, meaning seat or chair. The cathedral is therefore, quite literally, the location of the bishop's seat and the principal church of a diocese. Until the Glasgow inquest, the episcopate of Bishop John (from around 1114 to 1147) and the consecration of the cathedral on 7 July 1136, there is no evidence for the existence of such a church or community of clergy.

The barony helped finance Bishop Jocelin's rebuilding of the cathedral after a fire around 1189 had destroyed Bishop John's original.

By 1197 rebuilding work on the cathedral was sufficiently advanced for the building to be re-consecrated by Jocelin, around the time of Glasgow Fair, around 6 July 1197. Successive bishops, especially William de Bondington,

30 Ian Cowan edited by James Kirk, *The Medieval Church in Scotland* (Edinburgh, 1995)

RIGHT
Stained glass featuring bust of Virgin Mary, England, 15th century

BELOW
Seal of James Beaton (1509-22)

BELOW RIGHT
Tryptich of the Last Judgement (detail showing leper), Barend Van Orley, early 16th century

successors to have a fair at Glasgow, for eight full days from the octaves of St Peter and St Paul (7 July) – the celebrated Glasgow Fair.

It was not unusual for parishes to predate the formal erection of a burgh. Other examples within the Glasgow diocese were Lanark, Peebles, Kirkintilloch and probably also Renfrew. The foundation of the parochial system was virtually complete by 1274 when the first taxation roll of Scottish benefices appears. In general the pattern established by the close of the twelfth century continued well beyond the sixteenth century.

Friaries – preaching and teaching

With the coming of the friars, urban Glasgow saw the development of religious orders. These friaries, the best-known being those established by St Dominic and St Francis, marked a departure from previous models of medieval religious life. Previously, building upon the rule established by St Benedict, religious orders had tended to stress a rural environment, husbandry and a contemplative way of life. By contrast, the friars sought out the urban centres of Europe.

The Dominicans (known as the Order of Preachers and also as Blackfriars) were the first to arrive in Glasgow and received land on the east side of High Street. A papal bull of 10 July 1246 granted an indulgence to all the faithful who contributed to the completion of the church which the Friars Preachers of Glasgow had begun to build.

Such education as existed, whether song schools, grammar or high schools was, for most of the medieval period, the responsibility of the church. Most teachers and university staff were churchmen, with the chancellor granting licences to teach. The association between the Dominicans and universities was forged at the very outset of the order's life. In Glasgow, a 'studium generale',

encouraged both by King James II and Bishop Turnbull, was authorised by a bull from Pope Nicholas V on 7 January 1451.

Having himself been a student at Louvain, Bishop Turnbull would have been well aware of the connections between the university and the Dominican priory there. This may have influenced the choice of the Dominicans' chapter house, which was also the friars' classroom, for the inauguration of Glasgow University in 1451.

In its early years the university was poor and the teaching of theology appears to have been fairly erratic. The arts faculty was the most secure and well-endowed in this period. Dominicans patronised their own arts schools rather than attending secular ones. Dominicans are not mentioned in the university records until 1457 and thereafter none were involved until 1470. Possibly the friars had no suitable students or perhaps, though keen to support and nurture the new university, in this early period attendance there was not for them.

A group of Franciscan Observants arrived in Glasgow some two centuries after the Dominicans had established their priory. When the Franciscans (also known as Greyfriars) decided to settle in Glasgow, sometime between 1472 and 1477, most of the land on the west side of High Street had already been fued out. The Franciscans determined to develop their friary on a substantial piece of ground which did not front onto the High Street, but lay slightly behind, along the line of Shuttle Street. Although their church and friary are long gone the distinctive shape of the friary land is still readily identifiable on a map.

A mission for caring

The work of the medieval church extended to the care of the poor and the sick. In the middle ages the term 'hospital' was wide-ranging. Some hospitals only provided rest for travellers while others cared for orphans, the

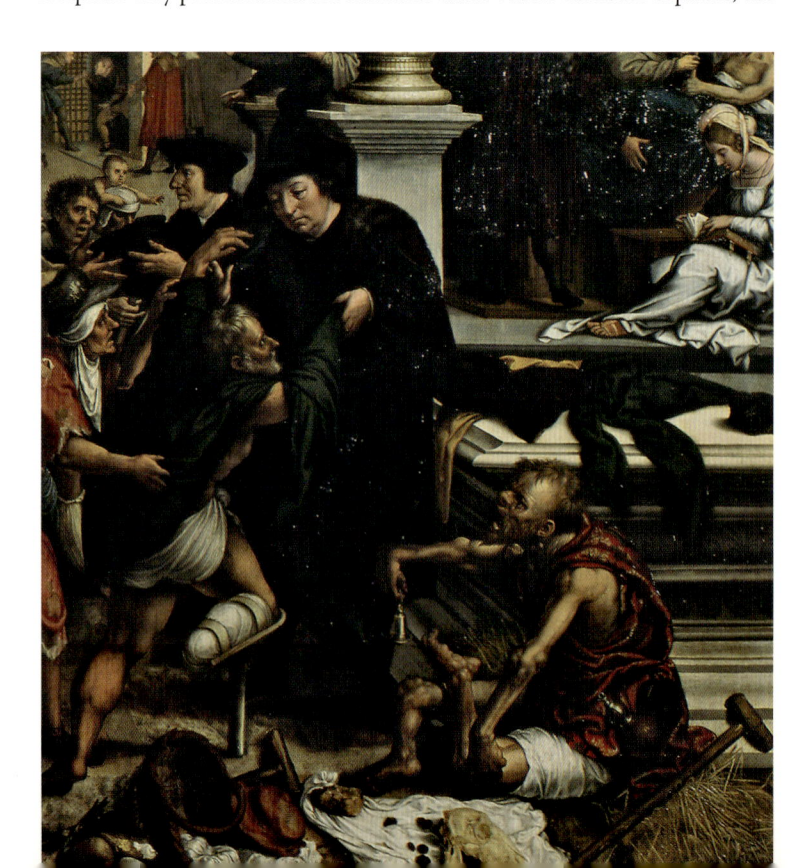

44

elderly or sick. Medieval communities took their duties to the poor seriously, believing that they would be closely questioned at the last judgement. Provision for the poor included offerings and collections. Almoners were appointed by kings and bishops to administer assistance to the poor on their behalf.

In Glasgow St Nicholas Hospital, founded by Bishop Andrew Muirhead, is central to the ongoing debate about whether Provan Hall in Easterhouse, or Provand's Lordship at 3-7 Castle Street, near the medieval cathedral, is the oldest house in Glasgow. It seems they may have been built at around the same time.

The claimed link between Provand's Lordship, and Provan Hall derives from the requirement on canon prebendaries to have a town residence near the cathedral. The manse of the prebendary of Barlanark or Provan is usually said to have been in the Kirkgait on the west side of High Street. However all the available evidence links Provand's Lordship with St Nicholas Hospital rather than with Provan Hall.

St Nicholas Hospital was located close to the cathedral. However for other hospitals a bridge end was often a favoured site. Lepers, the feared outcasts of medieval society, would certainly be lodged at the edge of town. St Ninian's leper hospital was located outwith the city limits at the south end of Glasgow bridge. It is claimed to have been founded around 1350, but may have been established in the fifteenth century, as one of the earliest references to male and female lepers in the hospital, and poor lepers dwelling there, occurs in 1485.

By the fifteenth century it was generally agreed that regulation of hospitals was important and a regime of inspection of their property and revenues was introduced. By 1549 a council of the Scottish church took episcopal visitation of hospitals for granted. In 1552 deans were ordered to include hospitals in their visitations.

By the sixteenth century plague victims would petition at the chapel of St Roche. In Glasgow the most common form of the saint's name was Rollack or Rollox. Like lepers, plague victims were housed outwith the burgh limits. In 1506 Sir Andrew Birrell arranged for a property in Ratounraw (Rottenrow) to house Sir Thomas Forbes, who had initially been appointed chaplain of the proposed church of St Roche. In 1508, Thomas Muirhead, canon of Glasgow and rector of Stobo, generously endowed the chapel so that mass might be offered for his soul as the founder.

A document dated 10 October 1508, appoints Sir Alexander Robertone to be chaplain of St Rollox. The transaction took place in the presence of two canons of the Cathedral, "and vicars-general of the most reverend father in Christ, Robert, Archbishop of Glasgow, being abroad".[31] The archbishop referred to was Robert Blacader, who, having been appointed bishop of Glasgow in 1483, was to become Glasgow's first archbishop on 9 January 1492. He died on his way to the Holy Land on 28 July 1508.

Drawing to a close

THE CAUSES AND EFFECTS of the religious upheavals of the sixteenth century are beyond the scope of this book. However some of the problems which beset Glasgow's church community over its early centuries, like the much criticised practice of appropriation, no doubt contributed. The Reformation forced Glasgow's last archbishop, James Beaton, into exile in Paris although there is still evidence of his interest and involvement in matters at home. His death there in 1603 effectively brings the story of Glasgow's medieval church to an end.

ABOVE
Carved stone fragment, Jedburgh Abbey

31 *Charters and Documents of Glasgow*, British History Online – www.british-history.ac.uk (University of London)

crofts and common meadows provided pasturage for animals and timber for

fuel

A Tale of Two Towns

DR E PATRICIA DENNISON

The City of Glasgow about 1547

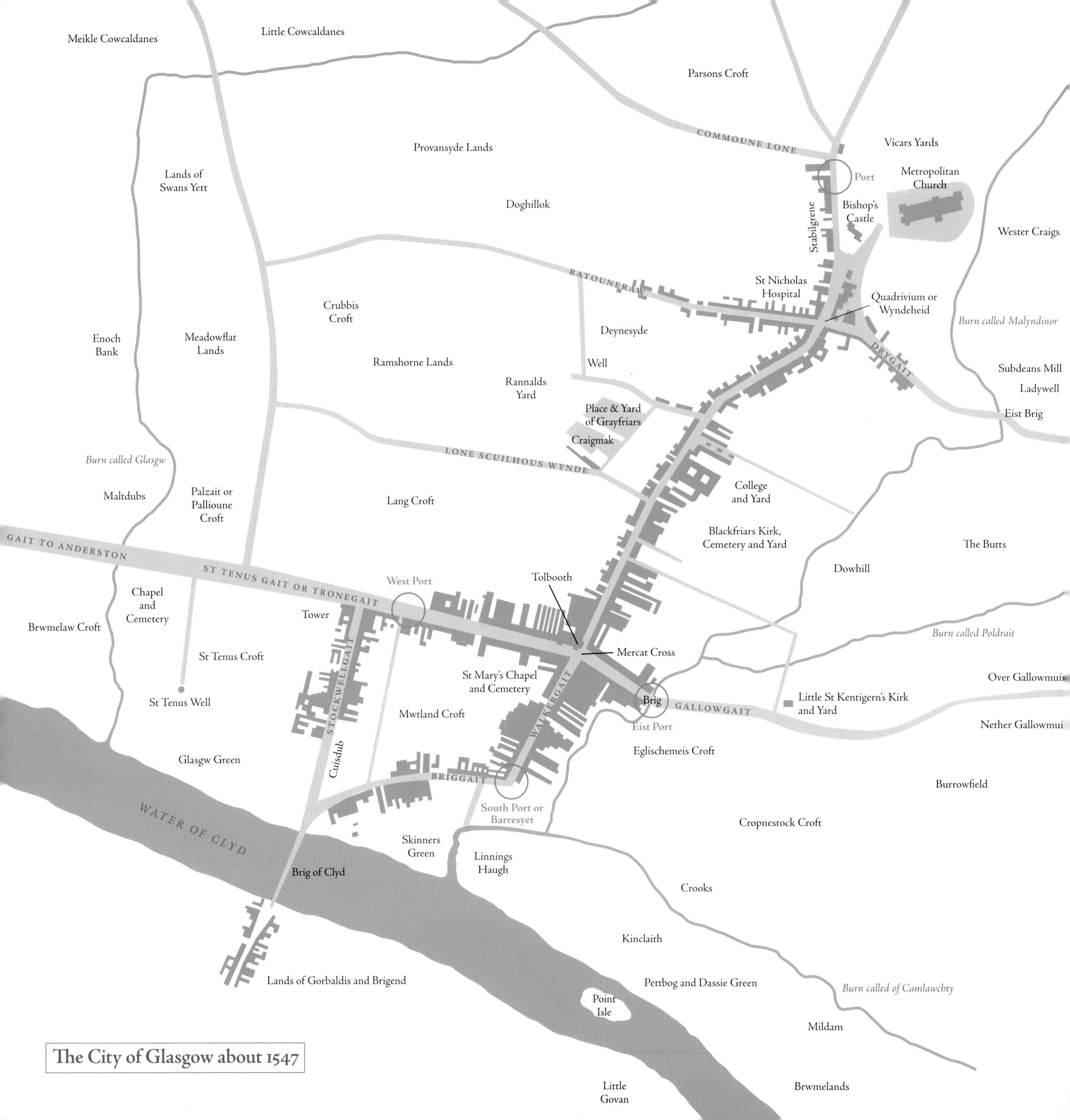

Glasgow's medieval history and topography were unusual. There were two settlements. One of these two centres was the religious area dedicated to St Kentigern (Mungo), focused on the enormous Gothic cathedral. The lower town was the trading area to the south that became the hub of a strong mercantile entrepôt. This southern township would, in time, make Glasgow an important centre of commerce. So, how did this odd configuration come about?

Early settlement

As far as we know, the Glasgow settlement became established at the northerly site of a church, or monastery. According to tradition, in the late sixth or early seventh century, St Kentigern founded a monastery at the same spot where St Ninian had consecrated a cemetery. It was here that St Kentigern was buried. Again, according to tradition, in due course this monastery was raised to the seat of a bishopric.

In fact, more convincing arguments might be given for Govan or Hoddam (in present day Dumfries and Galloway) being the episcopal centre. But the important point for Glasgow is that, by the early twelfth century, whether myth or fact, these legends were believed. At this time a re-established bishopric was centred at Glasgow and a cathedral was founded on the supposed site of St Kentigern's church – ground that was sloping, not highly suitable for building – but hallowed.

Glasgow's first cathedral was consecrated in 1136. Building a cathedral meant the presence of a substantial, semi-permanent workforce. They, and the clerics attached to the cathedral, needed basic supplies and it is likely that a small market became established beside the cathedral. This market was given further potential customers in 1161 when Pope Alexander III decreed that everyone within the extensive diocese of Glasgow was to make an annual pilgrimage to the shrine of St Kentigern. A further papal bull in 1173 refers to Glasgow as a 'civitas'. Clearly, the settlement beside the cathedral was by then well established, with a market catering for both residents and pilgrims.

The granting of burgh status

Very important for the future of this small settlement was that, sometime between 1175 and 1178, King William I, the Lion (1165-1214) granted permission to Bishop Jocelin that the township should become a burgh. It was to have all the rights of a royal burgh, one held by the king, to have the privilege of a market every Thursday and the freemen or burgesses were to have the protection of the crown.

The cartographic evidence suggests that Glasgow's early market was just south of the cathedral and the bishop's residence. Eighteenth and nineteenth century maps reveal a triangular area, by then built upon, but probably once an open market area. Sometime between 1189 and 1198 the burgh was given a further concession – an annual fair – and before 1211 the king guaranteed his protection to all who visited it. This meant that the new burgh had real potential to become a strong trading centre.

For the townscape one of the most significant aspects of becoming a burgh was that the town's land was formally divided up into burgage plots, or tofts. In the case of Glasgow, this was effected by a town planner by the name of Ranulf who came from Haddington. His name suggests that Glasgow's first town planner was a Norman, somehow appropriate for a place whose later development would reflect a plethora of international influences.

Certainly, at some point between 1179 and 1199, the process of setting out the town plan was well under way. Bishop Jocelin donated to the abbot and convent of St Mary of Melrose, his former charge, a "toft in the burgh of Glasgow, Ranulf of Hadintun built, in the first building of the burgh".[32] On these burgage plots the first burgesses erected their houses, usually on the street frontage, leaving space behind for growing vegetables, rearing animals, building primitive workshops, sinking wells and making midden pits.

What is not clear is exactly where these first tofts were laid out. It is possible that they clustered close to the bishop's residence and the cathedral. This would follow the norm for other early burghs which were initially laid out beside a nucleus, be it castle, abbey, or, as in the case of Glasgow, a cathedral. By the thirteenth century a dual centre had developed, with tofts laid out closer to the ford crossing the Clyde. This area recommended itself for development, being on the cross-roads of trading and pilgrim routes. It was at this time that the Trongate/Gallowgate axis grew up.

A two-centred burgh

Glasgow thus became topographically a very unusual town. It had two centres – the ecclesiastical in the north and the commercial in the south. As far as can be known, the southerly settlement stood initially to the west of the Molendinar Burn and its confluence with the Poldrait Burn. Development did not take place hard up to the line of the banks of the Clyde and the Camlachie Burn as this was a flood plain and quite unsuitable for building in the early middle ages.

Finds from excavations to the rear of Bridgegate/Walkergate (later called Saltmarket) imply settlement in this area from the early thirteenth century onwards. Walkergate was also on the direct route to the ford. This may suggest the laying out of plots for development on this southerly site at the same time as, or soon after, the laying out of the northerly settlement beside the cathedral.

Within a couple of centuries, the early settlement in the south had expanded along St Thenew's Gate (later called Trongate), where two chapels

ABOVE
View of the Cathedral from the Molendinar, oil painting, early 19th century

OPPOSITE
Sketch plan of the City of Glasgow about 1547, from the town records (map dated 1894)

32 J D Marwick (ed.), *Charters and Other Documents Relating to the City of Glasgow* (Glasgow, 1894-7)

ABOVE
North end of old Glasgow Bridge, also showing fords on both sides of the bridge, etching by James Brown, 1776

were sited, one dedicated to St Thenew, the mother of St Kentigern, and the other to St Thomas. By 1286 at latest, Fishergate was in existence, as was a bridge over the Clyde to the west of the ancient ford. There was also expansion along Gallowgate. By 1325, burgage plots may have even reached the Molendinar. It was to be this southerly settlement that would come to dominate Glasgow's commercial life.

The upper town was characterised by ecclesiastical buildings. Extension and repair work to the cathedral throughout the middle ages meant a permanent workforce of masons, joiners and other craftsmen. Although dominated by ecclesiastical buildings, there was also a certain lay element – bakers, fishermen, fleshers (butchers), dyers, skinners and cordiners (shoemakers) were an essential lay back-up to the religious centre.

The tofts in the northern focus of the town, the records suggest, were not as closely packed or on the same scale as in the lower part. Rottenrow appears in the written records in the early fourteenth century and Drygate a century later. It is quite possible, however, that they were in existence long before that, being on the important main route from Dumbarton in the west to Lanark in the east. This route also led onwards to Blackness, from where Glasgow shipped its overseas exports and to Edinburgh beyond.

Linking the two centres?

THE FIRST FIRM EVIDENCE of development between these two centres comes sometime in the first half of the thirteenth century. The road leading down from the cathedral to the south, later called the High Street, slowly began to be developed. It is significant, however, that the Dominican brotherhood was granted land to the east of this route sometime before 1246. Friaries were normally established outside populated areas, just on the outskirts of settlement. Clearly, this area was still considered to be outside the town.

References to a house with a croft (a rural dwelling) besides the friars' property in 1270 and the vacant land opposite them around 1300 are a clear indication that, for some considerable time, the two centres of early Glasgow remained divorced from each other. Indeed, even into the fifteenth century, there was sufficient available land on High Street, for a college/university to be erected on the instruction of Pope Nicholas V in 1451. About twenty-five years later, there was still adequate unoccupied land in the area for the Observant Franciscans to be given extensive lands west of the High Street.

The town's defences

IN COMMON WITH MOST OTHER Scottish towns, Glasgow was not surrounded by stone walls. Walls that did serve to protect the townspeople were more like simple wooden fences placed at the end of the tofts – the heid dykes. These may have been reinforced with ditching. Their purpose was mainly psychological rather than defensive, and their importance was two-fold – to protect the townspeople against the threat of disease such as plague and to exclude unwelcome incomers who might attempt to buy or sell at the burgh market without the payment of tolls or custom dues.

To the east and south of the town the burgh was made less vulnerable to clandestine entry by natural features. The Molendinar occupied a deep declivity between the present necropolis and the cathedral and continuing south, ultimately provided the boundary line for the tofts on the east side of Walkergate at its southern end. The fluctuating confluence of the Molendinar and Camlachie burns, allied with the vulnerability of the Low Green to flooding, added a further measure of protection in this area.

To channel entry and exit and to provide further defence, town gates, or ports, were erected. These were shut at night at curfew and opened at daylight. They were also closed when danger threatened. Originally, these barriers were made of wood.

The siting of the ports has to be assumed from their fifteenth-century positions as there is no earlier evidence. The Trongate or West Port originally stood at the intersection of Trongate and the Old Wynd. The East or Gallowgate Port was sited on the west bank of the Molendinar in Gallowgate.

The South Port, called the Barrasyett in 1503, was at the foot of Walkergate, to the north of the junction with Bridgegate. This port gave access and exit to foot and vehicular traffic crossing the ford. The Bridgegate Port protected entry from the west by the north side of the river and from across the bridge but it seems not to have offered security to the town from entry by Goose Dubs, an area of the town which probably got its name as the location of Glasgow's goose ponds.

A series of ports also afforded protection at the northern end of the town. The most northerly was Stablegreen Port, which adjoined the bishop's stables, approximately where the Royal Infirmary now stands, just to the south of the present St James Road (formerly Dobbies Loan). To the other side of the bishop's castle was Castleyett, or Castle or Kirk Port. This gave access to the cathedral precinct and was also the main defence of the bishop's properties.

These ports were reinforced by another at the eastern end of Drygate, possibly at a bridge over the Molendinar. The Sub-dean Port stood between the Gyrth Burn and Drygate. Rottenrow Port stood at the end of Rottenrow, possibly slightly to the west of the present Weaver Street and protected access from the west. The evidence is unclear, but it seems that there may have been a further northern port which would have allowed the Townhead region to be effectively sealed off in time of danger.

Greyfriars' Port probably stood near the High Street on Bun's Wynd, the track leading westwards from High Street to the Deanside Well and the religious house of the Franciscans (Greyfriars). Bun's Wynd ran parallel with, but slightly south of, modern-day Nicholas Street. Along with Rottenrow Port, it controlled access from the west. In 1574 these two, along with Drygate Port, were permanently locked because of an outbreak of plague. Since other ports were to be locked only at night time, this may suggest that traffic through these three ports was not so heavy.

The bishop's castle was itself a defensive structure and gave a further element of protection to the northerly part of the town. In existence by the thirteenth century at the latest, it was reputedly built on the site of an earlier rath or Norman motte, possibly built by David I (1124-53). There is no evidence to confirm this, other than ditching in this area which might have been associated with an earlier earthwork castle.

The castle lay to the west of the cathedral and occupied an irregular hexagon about 180 feet (55 metres) wide and 300 feet (90 metres) long. Its defensive nature was reinforced by a drawbridge entrance to the north. Between 1508 and 1522 the whole complex was surrounded by a stout stone wall about fifteen to twenty feet (6 metres) high, with crenellations – very much in keeping with modern day notions of how a medieval castle should look. Between 1524 and 1547 a gatehouse was added in the south-east corner.

Glasgow; an ecclesiastical centre

THE RISE OF GLASGOW, topographically, culturally and economically, depended on its ecclesiastical importance and its relationship to the burgh superior – the bishop. The status and dignity of Glasgow was raised even further in 1492 when Pope Innocent VIII raised the diocese of Glasgow to an archbishopric.

Inevitably, the cathedral dominated the upper townscape. The ecclesiastical atmosphere was reinforced by the residences of the canons – thirty-two in all by the Reformation. By the fifteenth and sixteenth centuries the upper township of Glasgow, Townhead as it came to be called, was characterised by the manses, gardens, orchards, crofts and the vicars' choral chambers surrounding the bishop's castle and the cathedral.

A chapel dedicated to St Thomas had been built in 1320. It may well be the same chapel which is mentioned in a document in 1462 as the location at Townhead where a university procession was due to begin. Glasgow's plague chapel and cemetery, recorded in 1506, was dedicated to St Roche and built outside the city precincts. Reputedly there was also a chapel dedicated to St John the Baptist at the head of Drygate, but there is no firm evidence of this building.

ABOVE
The Bishop's Castle, early 18th century etching

Bishop's Castle Ruins by Hugh William Williams, 1812

The southern part of the burgh also had a decidedly ecclesiastical atmosphere. An early chapel dedicated to St Thomas probably stood outwith the town boundary at St Thenew's Gate. Archbishop Thomas Becket of Canterbury had been canonised in 1173. It is possible that early veneration of St Thomas resulted in this chapel being founded very soon after the burgh itself was established. It had ceased to function before the Reformation. St Thenew's chapel with its cemetery, well and croft were also built at an early date, supposedly on the burial site of St Kentigern's mother, Thenew (or St Enoch). Sited to the south of St Thenew's Gate this important focus of worship may predate 1295.

A chapel dedicated to the Virgin Mary (the Lady Chapel) was certainly in existence by 1293 and stood immediately to the west of where the first tolbooth is thought to have been sited, on the north side of St Thenew's Gate. This chapel may have served as a convenient place of worship for the townspeople in the southern settlement, rather than the parish church within the cathedral.

The collegiate church of St Mary of Loreto and St Anne seems to have superseded the Lady Chapel and assimilated it as an endowment. This important building stood on the south side of Trongate from 1525. Between the church and the street was a burial ground and to the south and west were gardens for the prebendaries. This site continued in church use long after the Reformation. The Tron Theatre, which currently occupies the site, is itself converted from a late eighteenth-century church.

The first reference to St Kentigern's Chapel, or Little St Kentigern's Chapel, comes in 1500. It stood on the Gallowgate. There was also, reputedly, a chapel dedicated to St Nicholas on the north side of Gallowgate near to the Molendinar, but there is little firm evidence for this.

The presence of the Dominican and Franciscan friaries added to this ecclesiastical atmosphere. A Dominican nunnery was proposed in 1510. Although money was bequeathed for it, the nunnery did not materialise.

The influence of the church was extensive. It controlled most almshouses and hospitals and until the fifteenth century, all the educational establishments in the burgh. One of the first hospitals to be founded was for lepers. It was probably built soon after the completion of the bridge over the Clyde and stood a few yards beyond the south abutment of the bridge, east of the southwards track from the bridge. As with the chapel of St Roche, the leper house was a safe distance from the town. This was the usual practice throughout Scotland. Adjoining the hospital was a cemetery. Even in death lepers had to be isolated. In 1491 a lepers chapel was built a hundred yards further south. Both the chapel and the hospital were dedicated to St Ninian.

Close to the cathedral, near the Stablegreen Port, an almshouse or hospital, dedicated to God, the Virgin and St Nicholas was founded some time before 1464. St Nicholas Hospital was not large. By 1567 twelve old men were housed in the fore hospital and four in the back. Here too there was a chapel associated with the hospital. In 1471 a manse was built immediately to the north. Centuries later this building became known as Provand's Lordship.

A further hospital was founded in the north part of the town around 1524. Dedicated to St Nicholas, St Serf and St Machutus, it stood north of the Stablegreen Port on the corner of Dobbies Loan. Its name commemorated Roland Blacader, sub-dean of the cathedral.

Provision for the instruction of youths was also the remit of the church. This was initially aimed at training young men to enter church service. By the fifteenth century, however, the town authorities were also playing some part in the educational process. What was probably Glasgow's first grammar school was sited close to the cathedral. However, by 1460 a gift of extensive lands near to Greyfriars' Wynd enabled a move to enlarged premises. A 'sang school' was intended to train choristers for the church and there certainly would have been one attached to the cathedral. There was another in the lower town connected with the collegiate church of St Mary of Loreto and St Anne.

The most significant educational building was the university. After its foundation in 1451, lectures in common and civil law took place in the Dominican chapter house. By 1457, it appears that teaching in the arts faculty was conducted in a building which would later be known as the Auld Pedagogy, on the south side of Rottenrow. About this time a tenement and grounds on the east side of High Street, just to the north of the Dominican friary, was conveyed to the principal regent of the Faculty of Arts. Building began quickly. By 1467 further lands were granted extending the university's grounds northwards and east to the Molendinar. This site would serve the university until 1870 and its move to Gilmorehill.

ABOVE RIGHT
The ruins of the Auld Pedagogy, c. 1860

Glasgow; a trading centre

As well as enhanced ecclesiastical status, the bishop of Glasgow also gained increasing temporal authority in the fifteenth century. In 1450, the barony of Glasgow, which included the burgh, was raised in standing to a regality by royal charter. This was confirmed in 1476. Although technically this was an honour bestowed on the bishop, it gave Glasgow increased status over nearby rival burghs, such as the royal burghs of Rutherglen, Renfrew and Dumbarton.

Further concessions from the crown followed. In 1490 the bishop was authorised to have an official tron, or weigh beam, and to charge customs on all who were obliged to weigh their goods there. Dockets were supplied, certifying that customs duty had indeed been paid. Importantly, Glasgow's burgesses were also given the right to trade and export overseas. This privilege was technically reserved for royal burghs but was also bestowed on important ecclesiastical foundations. The southern lower town probably benefited most from these royal economic privileges, being close to the Clyde and on the mainland route to Blackness and Edinburgh in the east and Govan and Dumbarton in the west.

The market cross became the focal point for Glasgow's substantially increased trading activities. There is no documentation to indicate where the cross was initially sited. However, from later evidence, it is assumed that it stood at the junction of Walkergate, Trongate and Gallowgate. The tron stood nearby. To the north-west of this market area stood the tolbooth where market tolls were collected and the town's weights were kept. There was probably an early tolbooth as this was an important symbol of secular power, although the first documentary reference to it comes only in 1454.

By the sixteenth century Glasgow had a number of separate specialised market places – a certain sign that the town was flourishing economically. Linen and woollen cloth were traded above and below the market cross. Fruit and vegetables were sold in Gallowgate. Fairs, much larger gatherings which drew merchants from far afield and overseas, were held on the Craignaught lands to the west of the High Street.

The success of Glasgow's markets and fairs depended on the skills of its craftsmen and the quality of the goods they produced. Many of them depended on the essential water source within the town – the burns. These were a vital part of the medieval burgh's topography. The name Walkergate suggests that fulling – or waulking – was taking place in the backlands on the east side of the roadway in the Molendinar waters. Tanning, which needed plentiful supplies of running water and bark was probably also using the same water supply. Dyers, weavers, skinners, cobblers, blacksmiths and, of course, millers all needed water.

In addition to supplying much of Glasgow's early industry the Molendinar also ran three very early mills. One of these was at Mid Dam, now incorporated into Glasgow Green, and one sat at the foot of Drygate. To the north of the town, Garngad was also considered one of the town's official mills. For a short while, in the fourteenth century, there was also a mill on the Poldrait Burn.

Just as the name Walkergate gives clues to the craftsmen working in the vicinity, so do the streets called Fishergate and the later Candleriggs.

ABOVE
St Nicholas Hospital c. mid 18th century. Etching by A Morrison, 19th century

BELOW LEFT
Blacksmith and linen bleachers, Stephen Adam, c. 1878, windows made for Maryhill Burgh Hall showing local trades and professions

Candle-making was a dangerous trade with constant likelihood of fire. Burgh authorities usually banned such crafts to the outskirts of the town. By 1560 the road where the candlemakers plied their trade had begun to develop, leading up from Trongate, running parallel to High Street through croft land.

Throughout the middle ages, Glasgow retained many rural characteristics. Outwith the town itself the burgh's extensive common lands were divided into arable rigs, where the burgesses grew crops to supplement the produce grown in their backlands. The burgh's crofts and common meadows also provided pasturage for animals and timber for fuel. Although the built up, or 'biggit' area of the town remained small, it was the nucleus of a community that depended for its survival on the surrounding extensive common territory, and beyond – on the vast trading hinterland of the bishop's barony.

The increasing prosperity of the burgh in the fifteenth and sixteenth centuries manifested itself in the physical form of the burgh itself. Around 1400 the population was about 1,500 to 2,000, rising to between 2,500 and 3,000 a century later, increasing to around 4,500 by the Reformation and to about 7,500 by the end of the sixteenth century. In spite of this rapid population growth, documentary sources suggest that the burgh expanded little beyond its early boundaries.

By the sixteenth century the town ports appear to have remained on their original medieval sites, highlighting the small scale of the pre-Reformation burgh. Candleriggs was still considered outwith the town. The net result was that pressure for building space around the Cross was intense. Development of further buildings in the backlands of burgage plots, a process called repletion, another sign of a growing population, is shown by the numerous small vennels leading to back premises. Surviving records indicate that Muthill croft, between Trongate and Bridgegate and further west, Stockwell croft, were developed in time.

The jostling for elbow-room within the confined area of the lower town contrasted with the much more measured and gradual development of the upper town and the cathedral. Ribbon development along the High Street continued. Some burgage plots ran down to the Molendinar on the east. The fact that the Dominican friary, the university and the Franciscan friary could all be set up on vacant land is a clear indication of the lack of development on both sides of the High Street.

These foundations, in effect, acted as a buffer zone between Glasgow's two settlements. The lands of Ramshorn and Craignaught lay undeveloped and there was waste land on the west side of High Street until the end of the sixteenth century. The fact that fairs, which required huge open spaces, continued to be held at Craignaught is sure indication of lack of development between the two centres.

Glasgow in the sixteenth century

There is a very little evidence of development in the upper town – at the top end of High Street – in the sixteenth century. The Reformation of 1560 was to bring change, although not overnight. The gradual departure of many ecclesiastics was to have the most profound effect. Increasing references to property transactions in the protocol books of notaries between the 1560s and the 1580s do not reflect the extension of the 'biggit' area here, but rather the disposal of former ecclesiastical possessions. Indeed, numerous references to ploughlands and wastelands in Rottenrow confirm the lack of development of upper Glasgow until well into the sixteenth century.

By the sixteenth century, when the medieval period was coming to a close, Glasgow was already making an impact as a centre of trade. The town was beginning to offer a large commercial contribution. However it remained essentially a small town. Its topography changed little throughout the middle ages. The basic street pattern remained unaltered but extra vennels and closes increased the density of the built-up area as the town attempted to house its growing population. It did not significantly break out from its traditional confines. And, as a new period of social and political change dawned, Glasgow was to be found as it had started out – a two-centre settlement.

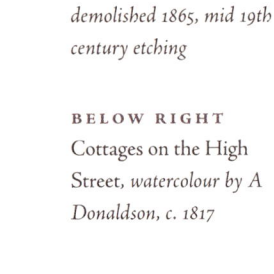

BELOW LEFT
Trade's Almhouse, demolished 1865, mid 19th century etching

BELOW RIGHT
Cottages on the High Street, watercolour by A Donaldson, c. 1817

ABOVE

Medieval High Street c. 1520 (detail showing burgage plots). Watercolour by David Simon, 2006.

not a
slate, tile, stone, shard of glass
or length of

timber

The Great Buildings of Early Glasgow
DR JAMES MACAULAY

ABOVE
Provand's Lordship with the St Mungo Museum and the Cathedral in the background

RIGHT
John Slezer's view of Glasgow, 1693

Sources

APART FROM THE CATHEDRAL and Provand's Lordship, there is not a slate, tile, stone, shard of glass or length of timber of medieval Glasgow still standing above ground. Virtually all of the original, two centred, town has gone – consumed by a succession of devastating fires, torn down by well-intentioned, though perhaps misguided, nineteenth century improvers or simply fallen prey to neglect or changes of use and fashion.

Yet the task of writing about stone and wood – of the habitations of ordinary folk, of religious houses, the first university buildings – is not entirely impossible. Medieval Glasgow can be rediscovered from archaeology, from documentary evidence and by making comparisons with other towns. Aberdeen was, like Glasgow, an ancient and territorially significant bishopric. In Aberdeen too an early university was founded. However some indication of Glasgow's early status is revealed by the fact that while Glasgow's university was founded in 1451, its Aberdonian counterpart dates from 1495, almost half a century later.

Recently an alliance of archaeology with medieval studies has helped to provide hard and fast information about, for example, the Franciscan friary. Latter day scholars have written perceptively of Scotland's medieval architecture, making it possible to assess Glasgow's buildings on a national scale. At a local level much knowledge and insight has been brought to bear on the history of the cathedral, its internal arrangements and the layout of the ecclesiastical precinct.

For antiquarians in earlier generations the visible remains of earlier structures were deemed worthy of recording either for their historical associations or picturesque value. So that Joseph Swan's engraving of the cathedral and the bishop's castle, "as they stood in the year 1790", is an unique record only a few years before the latter's final disappearance. Just as valuable are the depictions by Victorian artists, such as Thomas Fairbairn, of street scenes dense with housing. And, in the pioneering age of photography, Thomas Annan was asked to record the wynds and closes that lined the High Street before they were swept away forever by the City Improvement Trust which was more concerned with the possible spread of infectious disease than with the preservation of rundown housing.

The first known view of Glasgow is the topographical survey of Scottish burghs made by John Slezer at the end of the seventeenth century. His is a unique record. The panorama which he records shows Glasgow in transition. The layout, buildings, and remains of buildings of the middle ages are still identifiable, interspersed with the new university and mercantile structures.

The merchants' town

SLEZER'S VIEW CAN BE COMPARED with the near contemporary survey of Old and New Aberdeen by Parson Gordon of Rothiemay. Glasgow was similar in its dual origins, at the top of a hill there was an ecclesiastical settlement, to the south, north of the River Clyde, was the merchants' enclave. The road south was accessed by a bridge of eight arches, which rose in a graceful curve towards the 'Gorbells' on the Clyde's southern banks.

Not only was there a distinction of functions between the upper and lower settlements but there would have been differences occasioned by wealth and status. Merchants' and shopkeepers' houses were constructed with stone bases which carried jettied, or projecting, upper storeys covered with thatch. Trading booths would have been contained within the ground floor. The many, flatted upper floors would have been reached by projecting forestairs, as depicted in early nineteenth century illustrations Similar forestairs can still be seen in North Street, St Andrews.

By the charter granted by King William the Lion c.1175, later amplified by King Robert III, Glasgow gained certain trading privileges while remaining under the jurisdiction of the bishop. Nevertheless, the growth, albeit slow, of civic consciousness and responsibilities meant that, in time, there would be a tolbooth, perhaps by royal decree since it was King Robert III who

ABOVE
Saint Dominic, 20th century painting

LEFT
John Slezer's 1693 view of Glasgow University (1630-1660) and the Blackfriars Church (15th century)

had sanctioned the construction of Aberdeen Tolbooth in 1392 as both the headquarters of a putative civic authority and a prison.

Today, Glasgow's Tolbooth Steeple, stranded on a traffic island at the cross, is the sole remnant of the 1626 edifice. With its five storeys and a forestair climbing to the first floor, the Glasgow Tolbooth gave a good account of itself as the seat of municipal authority and prestige and an indication of the accrual of temporal power from the Church. However, of its medieval antecedent nothing is known.

The friaries

IT IS ONE OF THE ODDITIES of medieval Glasgow that there was no separate parish church, unlike Aberdeen, say, where St Nicholas' Church was the largest parish church in Scotland. The good folk of Glasgow had to trudge up the hill to the cathedral to dispose themselves as best they could in the nave.

In the course of time, a number of new religious foundations came into being. Some were of local inspiration, others a manifestation of national and international trends such as the growth of the mendicant or begging orders such as the Dominicans and the Franciscans. Unlike the monastic orders which were settled in the countryside, the mendicants were called to preach to townspeople.

The first of the mendicants to arrive in Glasgow were the Dominicans. In Aberdeen the Dominican house, the first of sixteen in Scotland, had residential and domestic buildings as well as a barn, a kiln, a dovecot, a garden and an orchard, all of which made for self-sufficiency. If Slezer's view is anything to go by, Glasgow had an establishment on a similar scale. Certainly the Dominican friary was sufficiently commodious that when King Edward I and his English court were in Glasgow in 1301 they could be housed in the conventual buildings.

An important role for the Dominicans was the preaching of the Word. For that preaching to be audible to the laity a rectangular chamber was preferred but with a rood screen or loft separating clergy and people. The church had five bays, marked off by buttresses which were splayed at the angles. Between the first and second bays from the west there rose a square tower in two stages, finished off with a spire and weather vane.

Slezer's illustration depicts a handsome edifice. However by the time he came to sketch the Dominican church in the 1670s it was already in ruins. In 1670 the building was struck by lightning, which, according to a contemporary account,

"Rent the steeple of the said church from top to bottom, and tirred the sclattes off it, and broke down the gavills in the two ends of it and fyred it".33

A new church, built by 1701, became the university church and survived until 1870 when the university removed to Gilmorehill and the site was cleared to become the College Goods Yard.

A late arrival on the Glasgow scene were the Franciscans, whose church and ancilllary buildings were to the west of the High Street on a site bounded by the present day George Street, Albion Street and Ingram Street. It was Archbishop Dunbar who provided the Greyfriars with a new church in 1518-32. The partial remains of the cloisters were revealed by a recent archaeological excavation, prior to the arrival of the City Science development.

Like others of its kind, as at Elgin, which is a rare survival, and Aberdeen, which was surveyed prior to demolition at the start of the twentieth century, Glasgow's Franciscan church was a single cell or rectangle. It sat on the north side of a cloister, infilled on the other sides with a chapter house and a kitchen to the south with water supplied from a well in the central green. In the decades after the dispersal of the friars at the Reformation all surface evidence of the buildings disappeared. Early in the twenty-first century only fragments of stained glass, carved stonework, the curved cut stones from the wellhead, the remnants of burials and some artefacts remained to be recovered from the site.

Chapels

EARLY GLASGOW HAD SOME half dozen chapels. St Enoch Square is a corruption and a memory of the chapel dedicated to St Thenew, the mother of St Kentigern. Just beyond the burgh's eastern boundary was the chapel of Little St Mungo or Kentigern. As part of Archbishop Blacader's policy of enhancing and promoting the cult of Glasgow's patron saint, the chapel was endowed during his episcopate. Again it was a single cell. The site was later occupied by the famous Saracen's Head Inn.

There was also the Church of St Mary of Loreto and St Anne. A hundred yards to the west of the cross and adjacent to the Trongate, the church was built to meet the needs of a growing population and to reinforce the faith of the disaffected. Sadly, there is no record of the church's appearance. The Tron steeple, straddling the Trongate today, sits in front of the original church site. First erected at the close of the sixteenth century, the steeple was modified in 1636. That the spire is a miniature replica of the cathedral tower gives food for thought. Was this an act of homage to the mother church or was it that late medieval Gothic architecture was losing its creative force?

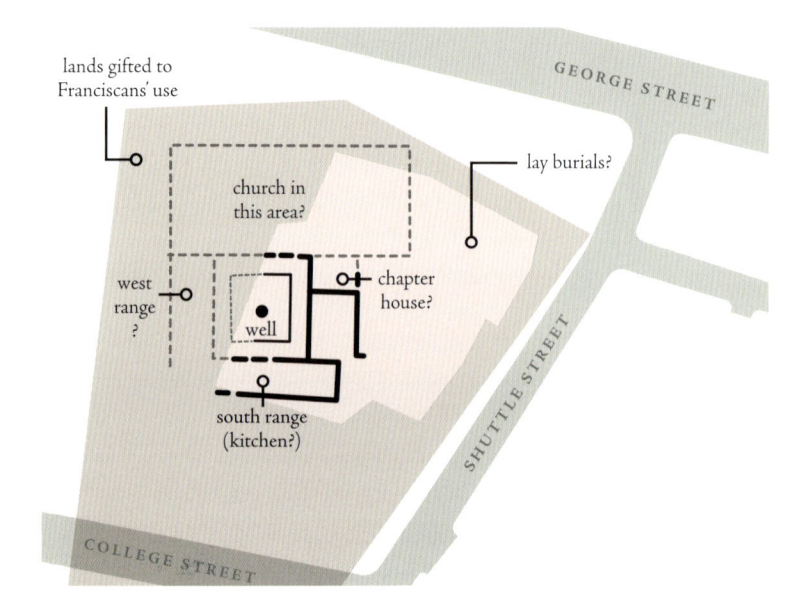

The grammar school and the university

EARLY HISTORIES OF GLASGOW indicate that the original Glasgow Grammar School, which may have evolved from the cathedral choir school, significantly predated the university. However the first written reference to the school was a deed from 1460 in which a tenement on the west side of the High Street and south of Rannald's Wynd (later Grammar School Wynd, subsequently part of Ingram Street) was gifted to the then rector of the Grammar School, Alexander Galbraith.

Over a century later, a council record from 1577-78 refers to the cost of straw for the thatched roof of the grammar school building. Further references record that the original building was demolished in 1600 and a

ABOVE
St Francis; Excavations at the Franciscan Friary site, 2004

RIGHT
Assumed layout of the Franciscan Friary

ABOVE RIGHT
Glasgow Grammar School (17th century), demolished 1874, painted by A D Robertson, 1860; University garden, etching by Robert Paul, 1762

33 M'Ure, *History of Glasgow* (1736)

new school erected by 1601, forerunner of the Glasgow High School which survives to the present day.

The major secular building in medieval Glasgow must have been the university, although it would have been tiny compared with the splendid edifice erected in the mid-seventeenth century. The founder of the university, Bishop Turnbull, obtained a papal bull in 1451, making Glasgow's the tenth oldest university in Europe. Tenements on the east side of the High Street and on the northern limit of the merchant city were granted by donors early-on. It is no coincidence that the first gifts of land, on the upper edge of the merchant city, were immediately to the north of the church of the Blackfriars whose brethren included notable university teachers.

There is no trace of the medieval structures although one can imagine that they would have conformed in scale and configuration to the quadrangular layout of the near contemporary King's College at Old Aberdeen where, uniquely, the chapel has survived. As one would expect, the chapel at King's is a single cell but terminated at the east end with the continental innovation of a three-sided apse. The other ranges would have included a great hall, doubtless for teaching and ceremonial occasions, and lodgings for the principal and students. In Glasgow there was the Auld Pedagogy with an upper hall, a teaching hall below and a small library.

The cathedral precinct

IN GLASGOW, ALL WAS UNDER the control of the bishops. When their rank was increased to archbishop in 1492, Glasgow vied with St Andrews for archiepiscopal supremacy within Scotland. With their territorial dominion reaching from Argyll to the Scottish borders, the bishops of Glasgow, often holders of high administrative office in the governance of the kingdom of Scotland, could afford to be great builders. Indeed, their prestige demanded it. Even so, each in turn had the burden of struggling to fund the completion of the cathedral. There were frequent setbacks, as when a major fire in the year 1400 meant that the upper stages of the central tower and much of the north side of the choir had to be rebuilt.

A notable builder was Bishop John Cameron (1426-46) whose achievements earned him the epithet 'the Magnificent'. Among other endeavours he gave the precinct of the cathedral much of its final form. Slezer's view depicts something of its locus which was comparable to the surviving Chanonry which still envelops Aberdeen's cathedral. To take account of the extent of the spiritual jurisdiction and the concomitant administrative duties of his bishopric, Bishop Cameron enlarged the chapter at Glasgow Cathedral to thirty canons or prebendaries.

In the early sixteenth century, the principal of the university lamented that "the church possesses prebends many and fat". Each of the prebendaries was required to reside by the cathedral for six months in each year, leaving a curate to fulfill the religious observances in the parishes. Each therefore required accommodation near the cathedral as did its administrative officials, all of whom were clerics and those, such as choristers, who sang the office.

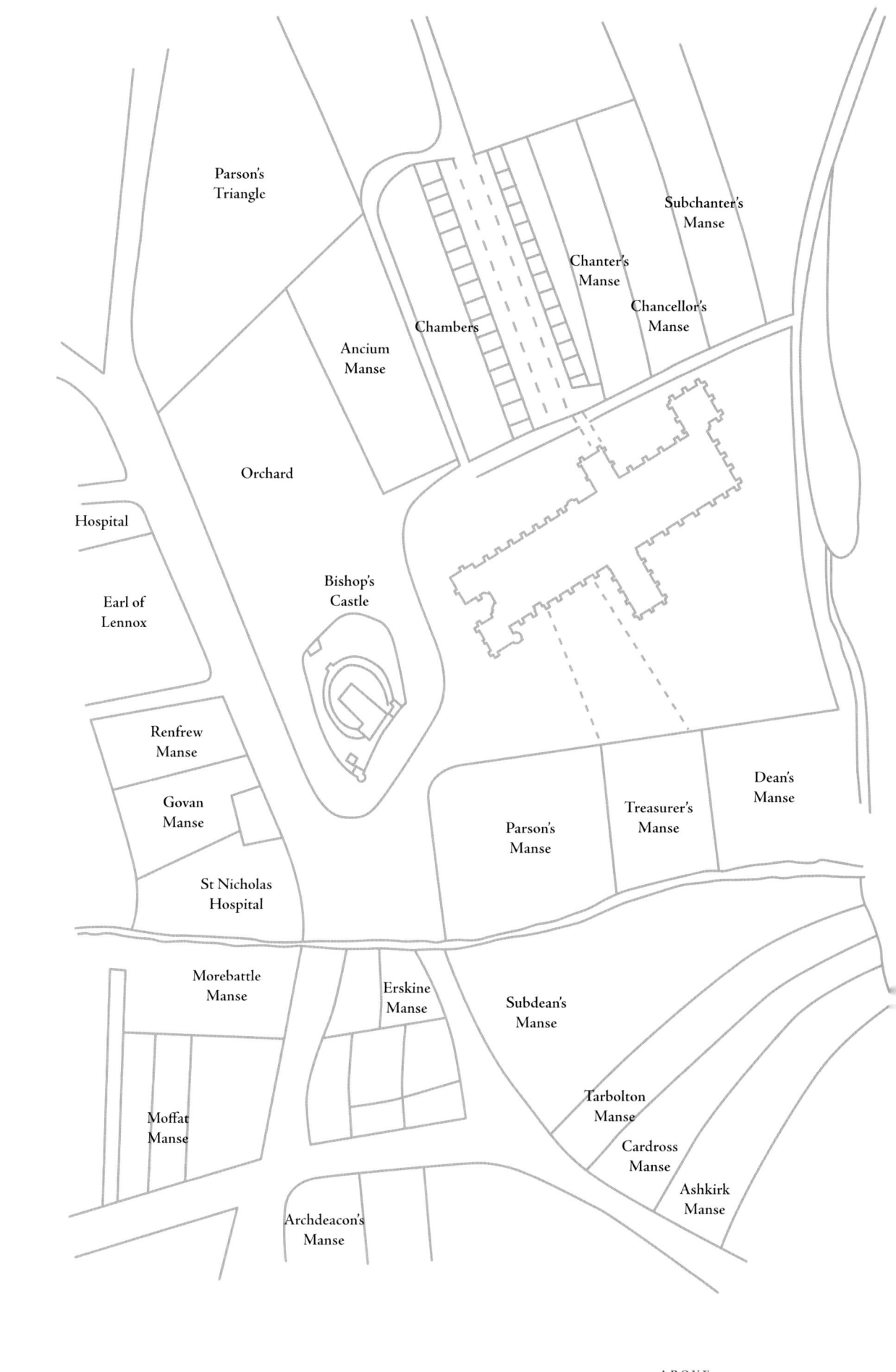

ABOVE
Conjectural plan of cathedral precinct for John Durkan's book on Glasgow Cathedral, 1986 adapted from sketch plan in Robert Renwick's History of Glasgow, *1921*

BELOW
Glasgow Cathedral and the bishop's castle, based on painting by Thomas Hearne, 1787

BELOW RIGHT
Historic Royal Arms of Scotland from St Nicholas Garden, Provand's Lordship. Lion Rampant set in the central shield incorporated in the reign of William I (1165-1214). Chained unicorns with crowns around their necks date from c. the reign of James II (1437-1460). The thistle (usually) incorporates the jewel of St Andrew. The whole surmounted by a crowned lion with sword and (usually) a sceptre. This version c. 19th century

BOTTOM RIGHT
St Nicholas Hospital and chapel and bishop's castle, c. 1780

To the south of the cathedral were the residences of the treasurer and the dean and to the north there was the chancellor's residence. In an arc stretching from east to west and filling the four streets around the cathedral were the other manses including the manses of Renfrew and Eaglesham. After the Reformation they were incorporated into the Duke of Montrose's Lodging and so survived long enough into the nineteenth century to be recorded in plan and elevation.

The building line of Montrose's Lodging was on the Drygate. There were two storeys and half dormers breaking into the wallhead. A pend gave access from the rear where there was a garden and subsidiary buildings. All that would accord with Provand's Lordship, erected by Bishop Muirhead in 1471 and the only one of the Glasgow prebendary manses to survive. Standing in Castle Street, immediately west of the castle and the cathedral, Provand's Lordship became attached to St Nicholas Hospital, yet another endowment by Archbishop Blacader, which provided accommodation for twelve poor men. Old views show that its chapel was apsidal with a bellcote. The residential quarters were extended on the west where a succession of small gables show the new work.

It would be a curious chance indeed if the prebend of Provan were the only one which could boast the survival of both its town and country residences. Sadly Provand's Lordship seems to have been given its current title by the Victorians, perhaps recognising the opportunity to create a romantic, if historically spurious, link with Provan Hall. Situated just a couple of miles westward of the bishops' country seat at Lochwood, Provan Hall is a substantially complete pair of houses from the mid-fifteenth century and later, enclosed by a screen wall pierced by gateways. Even today, surrounded by post-war housing and adjoining the Glasgow Fort retail park, Provan Hall still emanates tranquillity and repose.

So, what of the upper town which even today is still dominated by the cathedral? The best views are obtained from the south looking up John Knox Street or from the elevated height of the Victorian necropolis from where one can imagine the scene as Slezer saw it from what was then Craig's Park in the late seventeenth century. In the foreground the main subject of Slezer's view was the cathedral; the secondary one was the bishop's castle. Below and swinging south and eastwards was the curve of the manses. Even in the 1630s this was a spacious, comfortable area, a place of dignity and with gardens and orchards, bounded on the western perimeter by the turbulent Molendinar, flowing down to the Clyde.

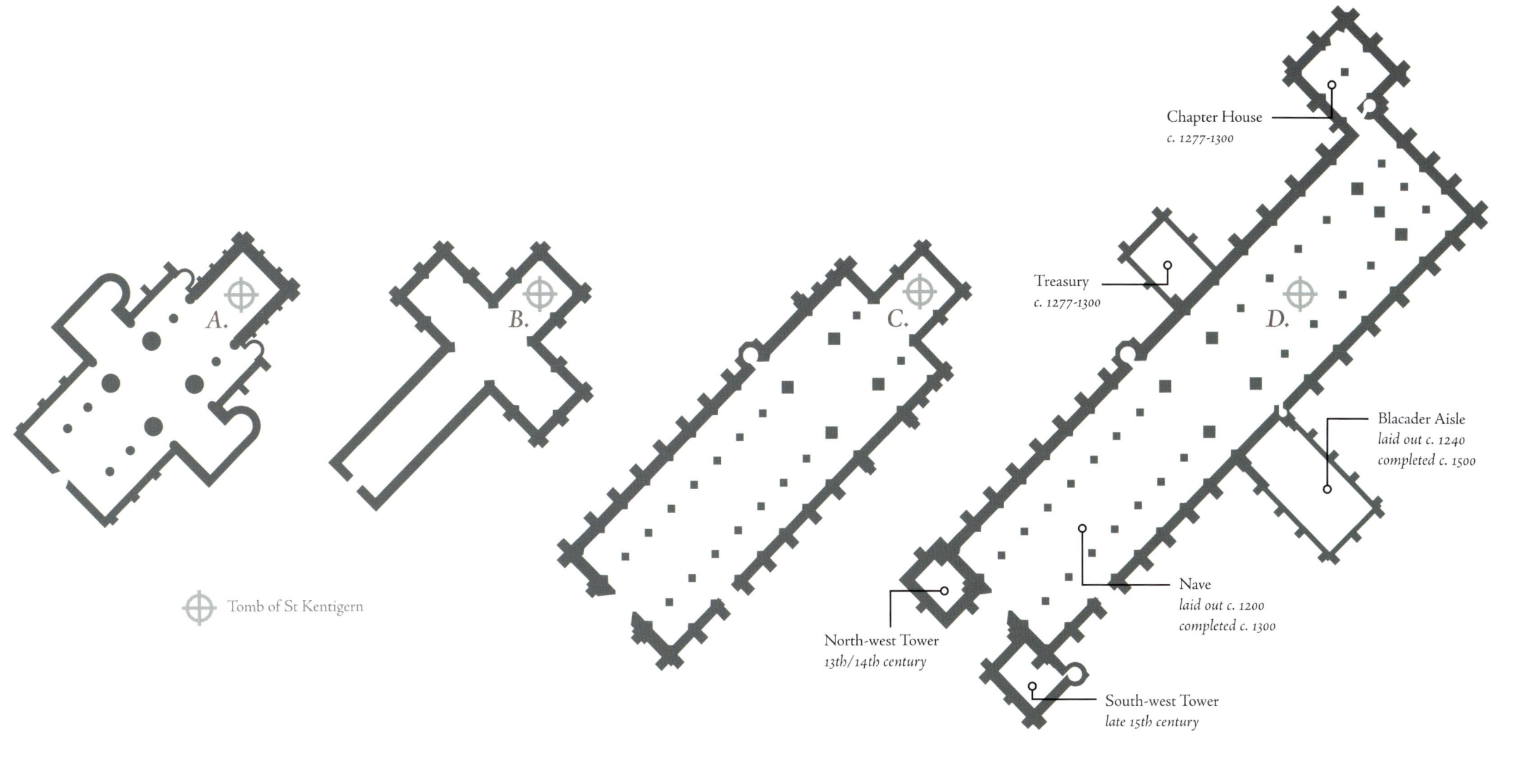

The castle

The bishop's temporal base was the castle. The present day St Mungo Museum occupies the western end of the original castle site and incorporates some remains. The castle was the burgh's main defence. Glasgow, like most Scottish towns, did not have town walls although there were a number of defensive ports or gates, controlling the routes into and out of the burgh. The castle was originally moated. The outline of the original ditch was discovered in the excavations prior to the construction of the St Mungo Museum.

The castle had assumed its final appearance by the late middle ages. Bishop Cameron erected the high tower which, with its battlemented wallhead, was like the towerhouse of any lay magnate. In the south-west corner was Archbishop Beaton's tower. The castle was pillaged in 1516. Perhaps in response to that attack a twenty foot (six metre) high precinct wall was built, topped with crenellations.

To the east, close by the cathedral, there was Archbishop Dunbar's gateway, a pair of towers with a caphouse over the entrance. It was embellished with a handsome representation of the archbishop's coat of arms. These arms are now mounted in the lower church of the cathedral. Such building activity indicated the need for security, especially as the troubles of the Reformation drew near. However the bishop's castle also represented medieval living in rather grand and palatial style.

The cathedral

Of course, dominating all was the cathedral, the fount of the bishops' spiritual authority. Today, it is hemmed around by the M8 motorway to the north and west and jostles, unsuccessfully on the skyline, with the massive insensitivity of James Miller's Royal Infirmary (1904-14). Yet, until the second half of the nineteenth century, the cathedral was by far the largest structure in Glasgow. So, how did its physical bulk encompass the lives of the canons, the merchants and the poor folk living in what would have been no more than sheds down by the river?

The site of the cathedral, albeit settled upon by folk legend and the burial of the local saint and undoubtedly problematic, was also in some ways extremely well chosen. The long south elevation, rising from the lower church, with the three towers uniting the parts and giving balance, rode the crest of the high ground majestically. In other respects, however, the site of the cathedral was less satisfactory. To incorporate the tomb of St Mungo was an essential consideration. Yet that was on flat ground, constricted to the west by a steeply rising slope and to the east by the boggy margins and rushing waters of the Molendinar, flowing from Hogganfield Loch to the Clyde. Such was the geography that would dictate the growth, plan and structure of Glasgow Cathedral for centuries to come.

ABOVE

Conjectural construction phases of Glasgow Cathedral, from Excavations at Glasgow Cathedral 1988-1997, *S Driscoll, 2002.*

A. *Bishop John's work, dedicated 1136*

B. *Bishop Jocelin's work, dedicated 1197*

C. *Bishop Walter's work, started after c. 1200*

D. *Bishop Bondington's work, completed c. 1300*

LEFT

Arms of Scotland (c. 1540) above Archbishop Dunbar's coat of arms and those of James Houston, sub dean, from the gateway of the bishop's castle

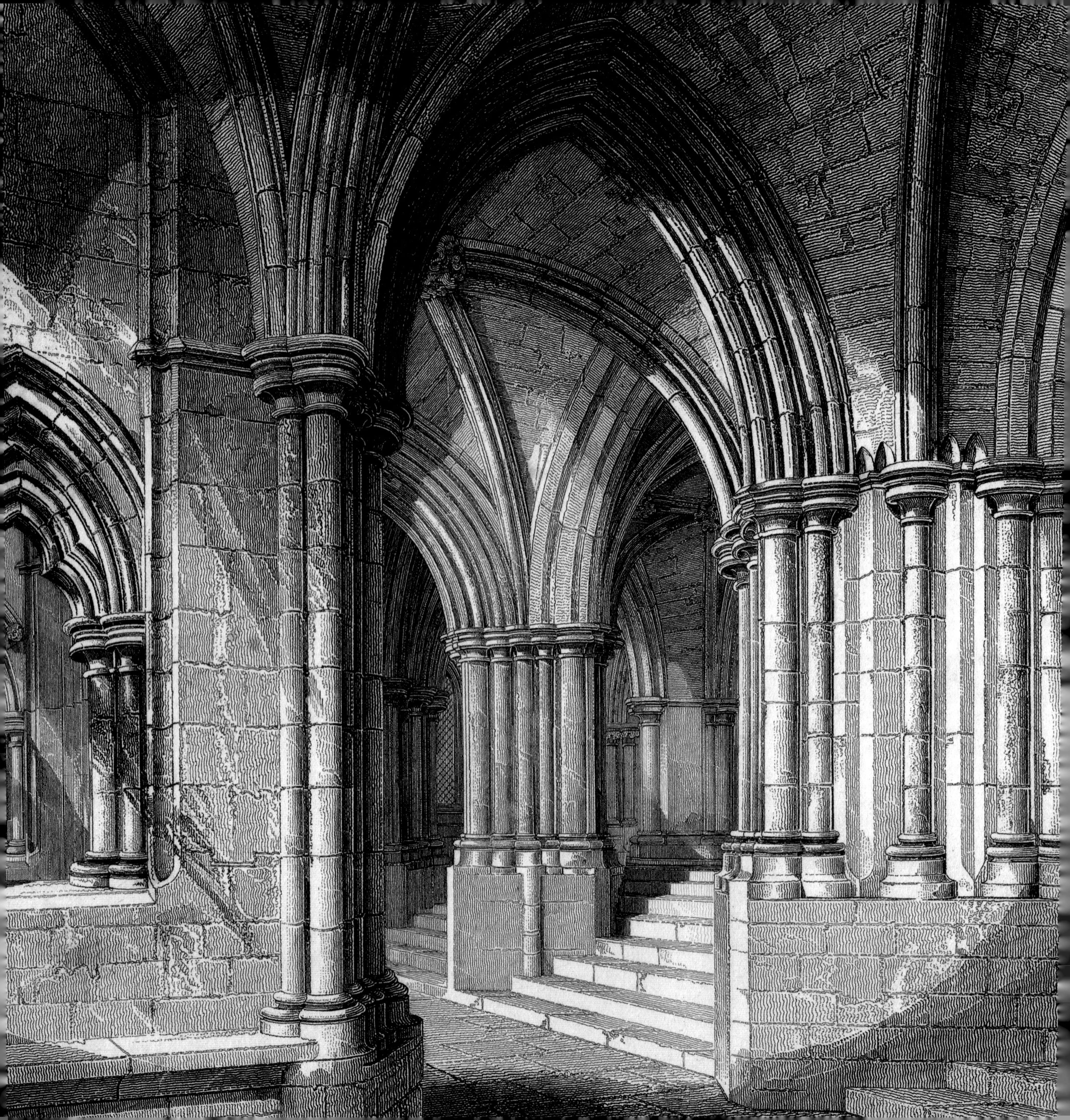

The first stone cathedral was erected by Bishop John, once a tutor to King David I. It was King David who brought the Scottish Church into line with the governance of Rome and under whom the division of Scotland into a network of parishes under the oversight of bishops was instituted. Thus, in the north-east, the seat of the bishop was transferred by royal edict in 1131 from Banffshire to Aberdeen and St Machar's Cathedral was founded.

In Glasgow, King David and his court attended the consecration of Bishop John's Cathedral in 1136. Almost to the day eight hundred and fifty years later, Queen Elizabeth II (King David's descendant) and her court attended a service of thanksgiving and rededication on the site of that cathedral. Glasgow's first cathedral extended onto the higher ground to the west of St Mungo's tomb. Thus a two-tiered eastern range was established which would be the pattern for all future building on the site.

Bishop John's church would have been in the Norman style, very much the vogue for grand buildings of the period. Round-headed arches were supported on circular piers with much painted decoration. Portions of this decorative work have been recovered from the site. However, in 1189 a fire destroyed the first cathedral, a common enough happening in medieval churches. Bishop Jocelin decided to rebuild, on a grander scale.

That church lasted for two generations. However, in 1233, Bishop Bondington began the building that survives. At 300 feet (90 metres) long it was the second largest church in Scotland, exceeded only by the, now ruinous, St Andrews. However Glasgow's impressive new cathedral was a long time in building, not assuming its finished appearance until the early sixteenth century.

Despite the span of three centuries, Glasgow Cathedral has a stylistic cohesion. Inevitably there are variations which mark the lengthy and interrupted construction period caused by lack of funds and, all too often, political troubles. During the War of Independence Bishop Robert Wishart (whose effigy lies in the lower church) was accused by the English of using timber to manufacture siege engines rather than construct the cathedral tower.

Glasgow Cathedral today is adapted to Presbyterian worship with the congregation seated in the choir around the chancel. In the middle ages usage was more complicated. The Cathedral was a great pilgrimage church and it was for that purpose that the lower church was laid out. Descending into the lower church by the north stair the pilgrim came first to the tomb of St Kentigern with its stone canopy supported by four columns at the corners of the tomb platform. Although empty, as his relics had been removed to a shrine in the upper choir, it was still a holy site.

The separation of the tomb and the shrine of Kentigern, and the importance of each, was recognised in a very public manner when King Edward I of England made offerings at both sites. Beyond the tomb was the Lady Chapel which normally would have been placed to the east of the high altar.

Overall the combined height of the lower and upper churches is 75 feet (23 metres). While Westminster Abbey at 110 feet (34 metres) is the highest uninterrupted vault in the British Isles the scale of Glasgow's cathedral was still impressively massive. The geological and topographical ground conditions of the hilltop site had to be countered. These problems were overcome by massive underbuilding at the east end of the lower church where the external buttresses are fed into the internal structure and the piers' great girth carries the upper choir. Even so, settlement has occurred in the south-east corner.

Glasgow Cathedral is similar to a number of French precedents in that nave and choir are a single enclosure with the transepts scarcely observable in the ground plan. To have built substantial transepts to create a traditional cross shaped plan on the awkward sloping site would have imposed great strains on the structure. Even so, a survey in the early nineteenth century recorded extensive cracking in the upper parts of the crossing. As a consequence the north transept was rebuilt.

Glasgow Cathedral is Gothic, the prevalent style for a grand church in the thirteenth century. The lower church and choir are in a restrained, unadorned style. The cathedral's acutely-pointed arches are characteristic of the first period of Gothic architecture. In the nave above, it is evident that there was a second major phase of building. The great west window and the upper stages of the nave arcade are both in a more luxuriantly decorated later Gothic style. Here, moulded shapes and softly folded curves of stone tracery are much more lavish than the spare, unadorned earlier structure of the lower church below. .

Many of Europe's grander cathedrals possessed twin-towered west fronts. Glasgow was no exception. Twin west towers were intended (but never built) for Paisley Abbey, which has many stylistic similarities with Glasgow

ABOVE
Details from Glasgow Cathedral – ceiling boss from Blacader Aisle; artisan figure; grotesque head; vaulting, east end of lower church

LEFT
Glasgow Cathedral nave

OPPOSITE
East end of lower church, Glasgow Cathedral. Engraved by J H Le Keux after a drawing by R W Billings c. 1852

RIGHT
Unicorn and dragon relief carvings, Blacader Aisle

OPPOSITE
Glasgow Cathedral from the south-west

BELOW
Glasgow Cathedral – view from the south-west engraved by J H Le Keux after a drawing by R W Billings c. 1852

Cathedral. The towers at St Andrew's have crumbled but twin towers still stand at Elgin, although much else there is ruined, and at Aberdeen. Glasgow's west front was unique however as the towers were not a matching pair and, rather than being in line with the frontage, they jutted forward.

The north-west or bell tower was square on plan with a timber and lead-covered spire. The south-west tower was used as a consistory or court house and held church records right up to the time of its destruction. Sadly, the towers were demolished one after the other in the 1840s in a burst of enthusiasm to improve and tidy up the Cathedral's silhouette and create an appearance more fitting to Victorian taste.

In architecture nothing is static. Changes are dictated as much by fashion as by practical considerations. Thus the stone screen or pulpitum at the east end of the crossing at Glasgow Cathedral dates from the time of Bishop Cameron and was designed to enclose the choir lined with the canons' stalls. To the west of the crossing was the rood screen, carrying the crucified Christ and the figures of Mary and of St John. The upper level of the screen was reached from a staircase in the north wall of the nave.

The central portion of the choir was enclosed by the parallel lines of the canons' stalls. In 1506, canopies were commissioned for the stalls, based on those in the Chapel Royal at Stirling Castle. Stalls, screen and canopies have all vanished. However a useful comparison survives at King's College chapel, Aberdeen where the wooden screen and stalls are still in situ and still in use – the most complete range of medieval woodwork in Scotland.

In the choir of Glasgow Cathedral, immediately behind the high altar, would have stood the shrine of St Mungo, elevated on a stone base, parts of which are displayed in the lower church. It was a setting of a type which can still be seen in Westminster Abbey where, because he was a king, the shrine of St Edward the Confessor has survived the centuries.

Archbishop Blacader seems to have been intent on transferring the relics of St Mungo from their second resting place in the shrine within the upper choir. The Blacader Aisle was originally designed with an upper stage to house the shrine. The aisle is notable for its collection of carved bosses at the intersection of the ribs in the low vault. These intricately carved and decorated roundels include both sacred and secular patterns. The instruments of the Passion are included as are the archbishop's coat of arms. Blacader's arms also appear on the altar platforms erected against the west face of the pulpitum. These altars, dedicated in the names of Jesus and St Mary of Pity, reflect the late medieval pre-occupation with piety. The altar platforms are rare survivals. They indicate something of the loss of altars and their furnishings which once filled the eastern chapels in the choir, the lower church and the bays in the nave.

In the middle ages the cathedral was crowded with altars which filled the side aisles and spilled out into the nave. Each altar had its own furnishings so there was a plethora of ornaments, screens and furnishings. It is little wonder that fires in medieval churches were such a common occurrence. Structural failure meant the rebuilding in the early sixteenth century of the north choir aisle where the vault bears the arms of Archbishop James Beaton. His namesake and great-nephew was destined to become the last Catholic archbishop of Glasgow. When the second Archbishop Beaton fled to France in 1560 he took the cathedral's treasures with him for safe keeping to the Scots College in Paris. In 1789, the turmoil of the French Revolution resulted in the loss or destruction of the relics of four centuries of Glasgow's history as a centre for pilgrimage and veneration.

With the departure of the archbishop much of the glory of the cathedral was lost. The cessation of masses meant that there was no longer a use for much of the building. The breakup of the diocesan system meant there was no requirement for an administration. Perhaps, therefore, it was fortunate that the choir, nave and lower church came to be occupied by separate congregations ensuring the building's continued use.

At the dawning of the Victorian era, the true value of this great building began to be appreciated. In the 1840s it was determined to restore Glasgow Cathedral to something like its medieval glory. Sadly, although much of the work undertaken at this time ensured the preservation of the cathedral's medieval fabric, the Victorians disliked the asymmetry of the original west front. As with so much the Victorians undertook, their restoration of Glasgow Cathedral might be admired for its zeal. However the demolition of the magnificent original towers, which had set Glasgow Cathedral apart from many of the great Gothic cathedrals of western Europe, was lamentable.

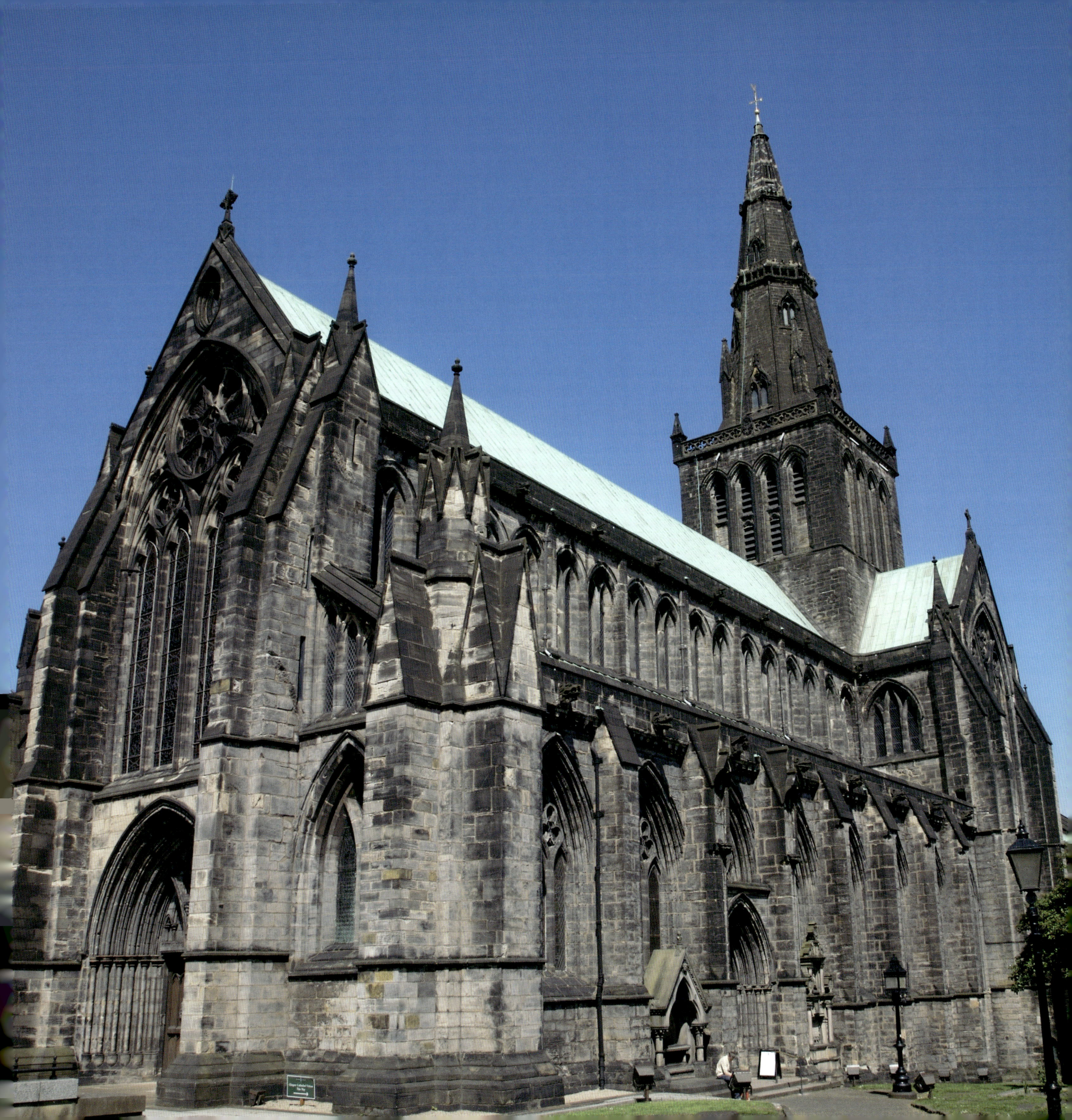

even a tinker would not deign to drown his

dog in it...

Daily Life, Disease and Death

DR E PATRICIA DENNISON

Rural origins

"Even a tinker would not deign to drown his dog in it"[34]. This was the damning comment on the water in Glasgow's burns at the end of the middle ages. Early settlers had chosen to make their homes near to the ford across the River Clyde and also further north beside the hallowed place where St Kentigern had founded his monastery. They had been attracted to an area that offered great advantages, including fresh, clean water. However, over the course of Glasgow's early centuries much was to change.

For much of the middle ages Glasgow was a rural settlement. The town was divided into burgage plots, or tofts, each with a dwelling at the front. The backlands at the rear were used to raise animals, grow vegetables, sink wells and dig midden pits. Subsistence in all small towns throughout the middle ages depended mostly on home-grown produce. The backlands played a key role in this. Animals were often free to roam the streets. Stables and barns were a common sight, even in the centre of town. Outwith the town itself, the burgh's extensive common lands were divided into arable rigs for the burgesses to supplement what they grew on the backlands; and the burgh crofts and common meadows offered grazing and a source of fuel – peat and wood.

The homes of the first Glaswegians were very simple – little more than huts. Made of stakes and inter-woven wattle, they had free-standing posts, just pushed into the ground, to support the walling – an insecure support in very wet weather. The roofs were thatched with heather, straw or even turfs of growing plants which offered resistance to rain. Doors were either straw matting or wattle and few dwellings had windows.

The interiors of these early Glasgow homes had basic floors of silt, clay or sand, probably scattered for comfort and an element of cleanliness with bracken, heather or straw. Most had the advantage of a fire, to cook on and for heat. The hearth was usually set on the floor as a clay-lined hollow or on a stone slab. Smoke percolated out of the roof by a small hole. These simple dwellings had no sub-divisions for living and sleeping. And they often housed livestock as well as the family.

Gradually the quality of Glasgow's housing improved. The free-standing support posts were reinforced by being set into ground sills of wood – later some of these were replaced with stone sills. Walls were made more secure and weather-proof by cladding with heavy clay, dung or peat. Some houses were then sub-divided with partitions, creating a larger space for living and working quarters and a smaller area for storage or housing animals. Only the very wealthy had separate bed chambers. Very few early Glaswegians were able to afford the luxury of glass in their windows, shutters being the normal way of keeping the elements at bay.

Throughout Glasgow's early centuries the vast majority of buildings were of wood. Stone was reserved for the prestigious buildings of the town – the churches, friaries and, especially, the cathedral and its associated manses. Provand's Lordship is the last remnant of these manses, but it has been so sub-divided since the middle ages that its interior bears little resemblance to the original.

By the sixteenth century, some Glasgow houses benefited from a stone ground floor with the upper storeys of timber. The wooden houses of wealthier folk began to have roofs of slate or pottery tiles, each tile overlapping the other and being fixed to the wooden sarking by nails at its top corners. The tiles on the ridge of the roof were often decorated and finished in a yellow, brown or green glaze. The vast majority of houses, however, were thatched – a constant fire hazard. It was only after the great fire of 1652, which left more than a thousand people homeless, that serious measures were taken by the authorities to prevent the risk of a similar disaster in the future.

The interiors of most houses were simply furnished. A table was one of the most important possessions. This was usually a board supported on trestles. After the meal the table could be dismantled and placed against a wall – an ideal solution in a cramped space. A number of the better-off homes had a compter. This was a reckoning table, marked out in squares so that money could be counted easily. This type of table was used mostly by wealthier merchants and craftsmen.

Chairs were not commonplace – they were used only in the most prestigious homes. The normal seating was wooden forms. Most people slept on box-beds, if they had a bed at all. Only the most well-to-do had the luxury of feather bolsters and beds draped with curtains to keep out draughts. Some households had sheets and bolsters, but for many the bedding was straw.

Early Glasgow homes were lit by candles or lamps burning oil, often produced from flax grown in the backlands. Most of the essential utensils, such as plates and dishes, were of wood or pewter and cooking pots were normally made of iron to withstand the heat of the open fire. Knives were an important part of medieval life – both for eating and craft skills. There were no forks – people used their fingers to pick up food. Most people had very few possessions so storage would not have been a problem. Wooden chests or kists were used and by the fifteenth century most dwellings had an 'armry' or cupboard to keep utensils and, probably, to display plates.

Work and leisure

Archaeological remains give us some clues to the leisure activities of the time, although working hours were long. The twelve hour working day started at five in the morning in summer and six in winter, everyday except Sunday, making the working week more than twice as long as that of the twenty-first century. After work, bowls, pennystanes and card-playing were enjoyed. Bone gaming counters and dice suggest that gambling was popular.

ABOVE
"Little more than huts... of stakes and interwoven wattle" – painting of typical early medieval house.

Typical Scottish medieval backland scene, painting by Jan Dunbar, 1997

ABOVE RIGHT
Scottish medieval horseshoe (13th/14th century)

Foot and hand ball, skating (skates were made from the metatarsals of horses), sledging and shooting practice with bow and arrow were common outdoor pursuits. Hawking and illegal hunting also took place. Gossiping and drinking probably filled many a dark evening – in that perhaps not much has changed.

Most trades, or crafts, had their workshops in the backlands of the burgage plots. The plots were divided from each other by gullies or wattle fencing, partly for marking out boundaries but also to contain animals. From what has been discovered by excavation, wells and midden pits were at times sunk very close to each other. Given that they were often lined merely with wattle, the likelihood of seepage from one to the other was high, with obvious consequences for the health of the inhabitants. As time went on, these backlands became less and less like kitchen gardens. Particularly near the centre of the town, development of inferior housing to the rear of the frontage building – a process called 'repletion' – brought congestion and overcrowding in the lower town.

The authorities were only too aware of the dangers of some trades, either because they were safety hazards or noxious. Some were banned from the backlands and placed at the edge of the town for safety or environmental reasons. The candlemakers' trade brought a high risk of fire – they were pushed to the edge of towns – in Glasgow to the area later called Candleriggs. Prostitutes were also ordered to ply their trade on the outskirts of the town.

Tanning was particularly unpleasant; hides were soaked in urine and gave off an offensive smell. Tanning works also needed a ready supply of water. They clustered along Glasgow's burns, which also powered the town's mills. The early name for Saltmarket was Walkergate, which means the street of the fullers, so it is likely that both tanning and fulling took place in the backlands of Walkergate and of High Street, both readily accessible to the waters of the Molendinar. Other crafts were dependent on this water supply – skinners, dyers, weavers, millers, bakers, cobblers and blacksmiths congregated, all competing for space, on water-fronts that were rather too close to the town centre and the all-important market. By the end of the middle ages the burns were heavily polluted and in warm weather the stench hung heavily in the air.

The market

THE MARKET WAS THE focal point of the town. The tolbooth and market cross, with the tron, or weigh-beam, were the symbol of the economic importance of the burgh. The noisy, bustling market was held on a Thursday

TOP
Building a medieval stone church (Aberdeen), painting by Jan Dunbar, 1997

ABOVE
Ice sledging

LEFT
Salmon fishermen and fisherman's hut, Govan c. 1815

until 1397 when it was either changed or added to with a Sunday market. Market day was later altered to a Monday.

Glasgow's early traders often had booths attached to the front of their houses where they sold the products crafted in their backlands. Others had moveable trolleys, rather like flat wheelbarrows, to display their wares. The local baxters (bakers), fleshers (butchers) and cordiners (shoe-makers and leather workers) were joined by others who had surplus produce to sell. Everyone within Glasgow's vast hinterland was obliged, officially, to attend the market if they wished to buy or sell, so market days were a crowded affair. At the time of the fair, held for eight days in July, many more thronged into the small town. Glasgow really was 'going like a fair'!

All those from outside the town who came to the market paid a fee, or toll, either at the tolbooth or the town's gates. The town weights for use at the tron were kept in the tolbooth. The weights were one of the regulators of food standards. All produce, such as bread, had to meet a measure laid down by the council. Ale had to conform to a set liquid capacity according to its quality. Anyone failing to follow these market rules would have the bottom of their pots 'dinged out', making them useless.

To ensure that the market acted fairly, and that purchasers received their food at a fair price, careful checks were kept on forestalling, the buying up of goods before reaching the open market place, and regrate, the hoarding of goods until the market price rose. Meat was also checked for freshness. However this was not usually necessary as the easiest way to transport meat to market was on foot. Slaughtering then took place in the market place. In this way the burgh maintained both quality and quantity control.

What was not controlled was the bellowing and mess that accompanied the killing of animals on the High Street. Added to this, fish gutting also took place at the market. Remnants of both animals and fish had several uses and little was wasted. Stomach linings and intestines were converted into haggis-type meals, sausages and tripe. Blood was made into black puddings, fats were rendered down for candles and soap, and bones were worked into combs, thimbles and tools. Scavenging dogs probably cleared up much of what was left, but conditions were very far from hygienic.

Public justice

AS WELL AS BEING THE FOCUS of the market, the tolbooth was the physical display of the town's authority. It was here that the burgh council met and where the town jail was located. The central market area was where those who had offended against Glasgow society were punished.

Jail and the ultimate verdict of banishment from the town were the most feared medieval punishments. Lesser crimes were met with discomfort and public ridicule – a time in the stocks or gowe, where the miscreant was held by an iron ring round the neck. The tron could also be a place of public humiliation – the offender would have his ear nailed to the wooden shaft. Women were placed on the cukstool, or if accused of being a 'scold', the branks, a crude brace, was forced into their mouths, preventing speech and causing extreme pain.

The purpose of all of these early punishments was to expose offenders to public humiliation. The best time to do this was at market time and in the market centre. There, anyone could come to witness the spectacle and, if they wished, throw eggs or rotten vegetables at the culprit.

Food and clothing

SO, HOW WELL DID PEOPLE eat and clothe themselves from their visits to the market and their cultivation in the backlands? From archaeological evidence, it seems that the most commonly eaten meat was beef, although pig, sheep, goat and deer formed part of the diet. Chicken and geese were kept on the backlands and culled for food and small wild birds were trapped. Dairy produce and eggs could be sourced from the townspeople's own animals or bought at market. Vegetables, such as kale, syboes, leeks and fat-hen (a nettle-like plant), grown on the toft, were supplemented by the collection of mushrooms and other fungi and wild berries, such as raspberries, blaeberries, brambles, wild cherries, rowans and elderberries.

The staple of the early Glasgow diet, however, was cereals – oats, rye, wheat and barley. These were all grown in the town crofts. Water was collected from the town's burns and also from water butts. As time went on, however, the water from the burns became polluted. They were a convenient place for refuse disposal, as well as the setting for noxious industries. Most people turned to ale as a safer source of drink, even for children, although the fortunate wealthy might drink imported wine.

On the whole, this was a relatively balanced diet – as long as there was enough of it. In times of dearth and bad harvest it was the poorest who inevitably suffered most. Winters were always hard times. Because of the expense of feeding animals over the cold months, most of the livestock was

TOP
Detail from Medieval Glasgow, mural by A E Walton c. 1902 from the Banqueting Hall, Glasgow City Chambers

ABOVE
Medieval long-toed shoe (Perth)

RIGHT
Silver penny of King Robert I (Robert the Bruce), 1306-1329; Copper alloy brooch, Scottish, 14th century

killed in early autumn, leaving only a small breeding stock. This in turn raised the problem of storage of meat over winter. The usual method of preserving meat and fish was to salt it and pack it in barrels. This worked to a degree, but meat often became rancid. To camouflage the unpleasant taste, those who could afford it bought spices from foreign merchants at the town's fair.

For most people, clothing was simple. Wool, canvas or fustian, a rough linen, were hand-sewn at home into skirts, mantles, petticoats, hose, breeks and shirts or sarks. Shoes and jaks, a simple type of jacket, were made of leather. Wherever medieval leather shoes have been recovered by archaeologists, their constant mending shows that these were precious items. References in written records to imported silks and velvets, to furs, silver belts and strings of pearls are allusions to the garments of only the most wealthy.

Disease and death

THIS SIMPLE LIFE, IN CLOSE contact with animals, midden pits, refuse on the streets, the intermingling of industrial, agricultural and residential premises, and polluted water brought with it numerous problems. Diseases, some endemic and chronic, were rife in a time without antibiotics. Probably the most feared medieval illness was plague or 'pest'. Plague was technically not one, but several diseases, the most obvious being bubonic.

It is quite possible that what was classified as 'pest' in contemporary medieval records was actually another ailment such as typhus, which hit when resistance was low, for example after famine. Bubonic plague is described in the records as exhibiting itself in sudden epidemics. The disease was kept virulent by rats and other rodents. Black rats in particular preferred indoor to outdoor living. Wooden housing, easily gnawed, inadequate sanitation and soiled straw on floors encouraged these hordes. If rats carried infected fleas, which then bit and attached themselves to human beings, infection was passed on.

Scotland's climate also encouraged pneumonic plague. Cold and rain brought this form of plague not only as a secondary infection to bubonic, but also as a primary disease. This was passed on simply through droplets from the mouth, even by speaking, when it could carry two metres, or by coughing or sneezing when it could be transported three to four metres. Death then came very rapidly. The chapel dedicated to St Roche, locally known as St Rollox, the saint who protected those with plague, was an important landmark, just to the north of the town beyond the Stablegreen Port, in an isolated site, where plague victims were buried.

Leprosy, a common disease throughout western Europe, was only partly understood by medieval people. The Glasgow authorities realised that it was highly contagious and that the infected needed to be kept in isolation. It was a horrendous affliction, causing disfiguration, pain, the loss of toes and fingers and the twisting of limbs. However medical knowledge was so rudimentary that even someone with a serious attack of acne or a disfiguring skin disorder could be banned from the town as a leper, sentenced to a life of exclusion.

The practice in many places and perhaps also in Glasgow, was to place those afflicted with leprosy on a form in front of an altar in the parish church. He or she was then covered with a mortcloth, as if actually dead, and removed from the town. Husband and wife, mother and child could no longer communicate with each other – they had entered a 'living death'.

Glasgow's leper house was on the south side of the Clyde, near to the south abutment of the bridge over the Clyde in the barony of Gorbals, ensuring isolation from the town. The lepers were permitted by the authorities to come to purchase food for their colony, as long as they carried clappers to warn of their presence and stood down-wind of the healthy. Attached to the colony was a cemetery where the leprous dead were buried – even in death they were exiled.

Many other less shocking infections and diseases which marred daily life are known to the present day. Tuberculosis, smallpox, amoebic dysentery, leukemia, cholera, spina bifida and arthritis were all familiar. Even the common cold, caries and gingivitis brought much greater suffering than they would today. But there was a further serious health problem that faced many medieval townspeople. As a result of close contact with animals, many people contracted parasitic worms, such as trichuris and ascaris, which might grow up to half a metre long. Travelling from the small intestine through the blood system to the liver, heart, lungs and trachea, they not only caused immediate distress but also reduced resistance to other illnesses.

Although constant exposure to a series of diseases could bring a level of immunity to infection, increasing mobility brought contact with new types of bacteria. One epidemic that hit Scotland in the late fifteenth century was a new form of venereal disease – syphilis, called at the time 'gore' or 'grangore'. It arrived in Glasgow in 1498, having first been recorded in Aberdeen the previous year.

There were attempts to counteract poor health and filth. Archaeological and documentary evidence shows that people did try to improve their living conditions. Cobbling made the roads and vennels less likely to degenerate into quagmires in wet weather. Wooden battening was sometimes placed in sodden areas, such as latrines, and moss was used as lavatory paper. The raising of interior floor levels above the muddy exterior did something to encourage cleanliness. Wealthier homes might even have had a pottery or metal jug in the shape of an animal called an aquamanile for washing hands between the courses of meals.

LEFT
Stained glass of kneeling youth snaring bird, English, 15th century

BELOW
Medieval dentistry from an illuminated manuscript; jaw with teeth and abcess; lower jaw with caries

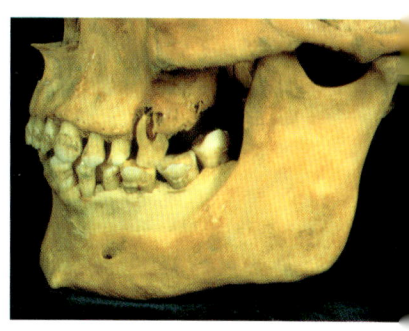

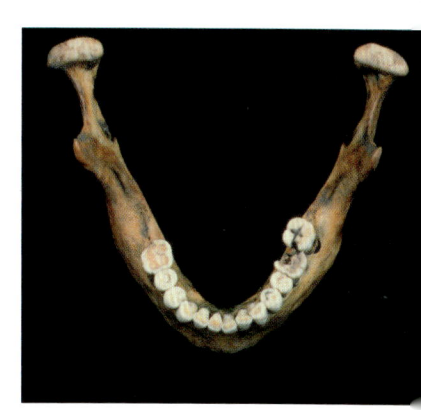

BELOW
Stained glass medallion with bust of young monk wearing black skull cap, white fur cape and purple mantle, hands raised in prayer. English, 15th century

OPPOSITE
Franco-Netherlandish tapestry, heron hunt, early 16th century

The town authorities attempted to improve sanitation, by ordering the removal of middens from the streets. However the fact that this order had to be repeated on numerous occasions suggests that little attention was paid. The foulness of the burns became an increasing problem. The Molendinar was particularly unpleasant, polluted by tanning and other industries.

The solution to disease and infection had to be self-help. Although there were hospitals and almshouses in the town they were not genuinely open to all and could accommodate very few. Archaeological evidence has shown the types of medication taken. Figs were imported, probably bought at the town fair. They were possibly used as a purgative.

Seeds of the opium poppy were taken as a sedative and poppyhead tea may also have been given to children during teething. Atropa belladonna (deadly nightshade) was cultivated as a muscle relaxant, as was hyoscyamus niger (henbane) which induced sleep and, if taken in large quantities, hallucinations. Other types of plants were collected in the wild for their medicinal properties. Over time, knowledge improved but life remained short and the spectre of death was constant.

The most vulnerable in Glasgow's society were the poor, especially women of child-bearing age and young children. Death in infancy was common. Health problems faced by babies today often proved fatal in the middle ages. Those that survived were weaned at around eighteen months and so the child lost many of the immunities gained from the mother's milk. It was also at about this stage that little ones became mobile and, as a result, vulnerable to the dangers of midden heaps and the filth of the town.

Such late weaning also put physical pressure on the mother, especially if she became pregnant while still breast-feeding, which in itself was not a secure contraceptive. For many women, life was one long pregnancy. Only a small minority of children lived into adulthood. It has been estimated that only about a third of women survived this stressful period of their lives. However, if they did, they often lived longer than men. Widows formed a substantial proportion of Glasgow's population. Anyone who lived beyond forty had achieved a ripe old age.

Seeking salvation

IN MEDIEVAL GLASGOW DEATH must have held less fear for the privileged and wealthy. Those with money to pay could gain spiritual comfort by buying masses, or even by establishing chaplainries, to lessen time in purgatory – the place to which souls went after death to be purified of sin before entering heaven. Consequently an important element of fraternal life for the guild merchant and the crafts was the foundation of co-operative chaplainries. These were, in effect, a medieval form of funeral club.

The vast majority of Glaswegians could not even aspire to funding a mass. It is impossible to know whether the prospect of the after-life perturbed the thoughts and lives of the humbler people of Glasgow. Perhaps the thought of purgatory was merely a further burden, probably best ignored, in what was, for most Glaswegians, a harsh and brutal life.

One of the church's main functions was to ease the transition from life on earth to the after-life. It dominated all aspects of life, from birth and baptism until the last rites and death. The routine of every day was dictated by the church bells which rang out the time to rise and start work and tolled the hour of curfew at dusk. At curfew hour the town's ports were barred so that no-one could enter or leave. No-one was then permitted to wander the streets unless on legitimate business, carrying a lantern.

Even the town's year was divided according to the religious cycle of the church and its special saints' days. While these were of great spiritual significance, they were also one of the few times when ordinary people had a chance to have fun. The solemn processing of the ecclesiastics and influential men of the town, carrying their guild and craft banners, was accompanied by merry-making throughout the town.

St Kentigern's feast day fell on 13 January and was a time for great rejoicing. The Corpus Christi procession, held in mid-June, was one of the highlights of the year, with tableaux on carts paraded through the streets, showing important events in the church's history and calendar – Adam and Eve, the birth of Christ, the martyrdom of saints and the horrors of purgatory. Only holy days such as these and Sundays provided respite from hard labour.

The lives of the people of medieval Glasgow were inextricably connected with the life of the church. The cathedral, the bishop's castle and the prebendary manses dominated the townscape. By the early sixteenth century the church of St Mary of Loreto and St Anne was the religious focal point of the lower settlement. Chapels were dotted through the townscape and the important complexes of the Dominicans and the Franciscans added to the ecclesiastical atmosphere.

The friars played an important part in the everyday lives of the townspeople. They provided charity and practical help in times of hardship. Much of the learning for ordinary folk came from the friars who taught the illiterate townspeople by pictures and using the language of the people, rather than the Latin of the mass. They were a well-loved part of Glasgow life.

Boom town

BY THE END OF THE MIDDLE AGES life was transformed. Life in the simple settlements of Glasgow's early days was a distant memory. One major change was the increasing pressure of population in a confined space. There were about 1,400 people in the town around the year 1500. A hundred years later, this number had risen to around 7,500.

Many Glaswegians were poor and living miserable lives. But Glasgow was a vibrant, hard-working city. The craftsmen were swelling their numbers and their output. Glasgow's markets and fairs attracted many from far and wide. Its merchants were bringing in great wealth and, by the end of the sixteenth century, Glasgow's economy was booming. This economic upsurge came at a high price – overcrowding, rampant disease and pollution. One of the key assets of early Glasgow – its clean water supply – was long gone. The tinker's dog was not the only potential casualty of a boom town.

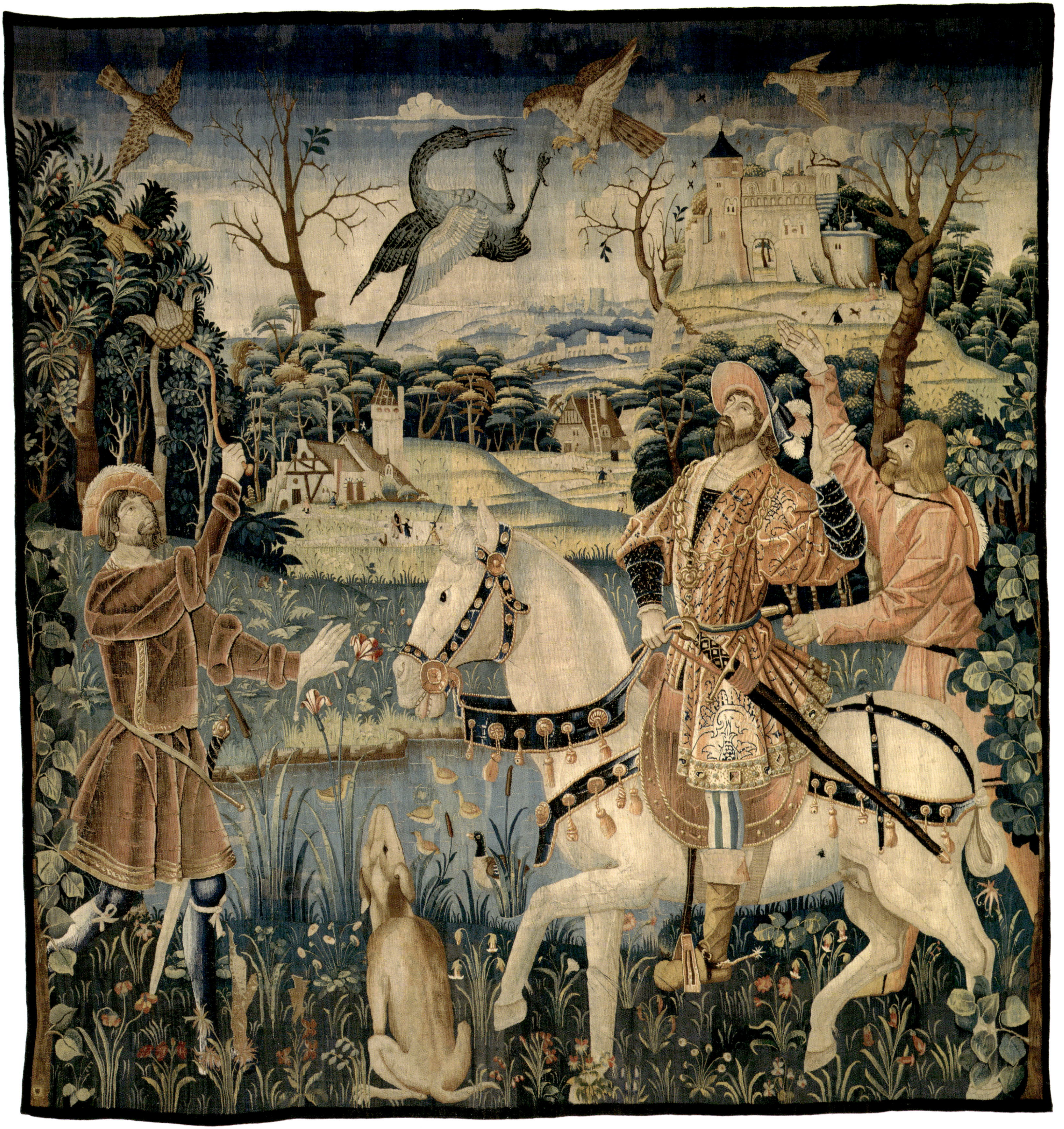

it is the smell that hits you first - a putrid, pungent,

pong

The Glasgow Tales

DONNY O'ROURKE

Contemporary reflections

Victor Hugo's observation that "In the middle ages, men had no great thoughts which they did not write down in stone", reflects the sense of awe and mystery evoked by the few European cities which retain much of their medieval built fabric. Places where substantial medieval heritage survives undoubtedly enjoy bolstered tourism and civic self esteem. The historic centres of ancient cities do not merely evoke the middle ages: to stroll feelingly through Cambridge, Prague or Ravenna is to have a real sense of what it was like to have been alive in the middle ages. Given Glasgow's history of reinvention and of tearing down its past, visitors to Glasgow need a little more imagination.

Of course the term, 'middle ages', was, like that depicting every epoch, largely posterity's invention. There is no doubt that some day the future will label our own brief time of breathing. The middle ages exist for us, they did not for those living at the time. "The Renaissance invented the middle ages in order to define itself; the Enlightenment perpetuated them in order to admire itself; and the Romantics revived them in order to escape from themselves".[35]

There are dangers in regarding the men and women of the middle ages, as being, 'just like us'. It is too easy to imagine our Glaswegian forebears on the basis of their dressing up box of tabards and tunics, doublet and hose. Conjuring up a nosier, muddier, coarser medieval facsimile of the present day with no portable phone, terrible table manners and even worse teeth. However, monks and masters aside, the average person had excellent teeth, being too poor to afford sugar!

Medieval paintings depict our medieval predecessors and take us back as assuredly as any TARDIS, as do the music of Scone's Robert Carver or the earthy ditties of the time. In their atmosphere and attention to detail popular works, such as *Monty Python and the Holy Grail* (1975), Ellis Peters' *Cadfael* murder mysteries, and Susanna Gregory's crime novels set in fourteenth century Cambridge, evoke the period well and are not readily contradicted by historians.

Amongst more literary explorations of the medieval period, Umberto Eco's *The Name of the Rose* (1983) and Herman Hesse's *Narcissus and Goldmund* (1930), summon up the spirit of the age with flare and feeling. Above all, the Ingmar Bergman movies that immerse themselves in the middle ages, *The Seventh Seal* (1957) in particular, capture the epoch's very soul. All of these musings on the middle ages feature characters like us but, at the same time bewilderingly not! Although none of these works of art is specifically about Glasgow the city was in at least some respects, a bit like that.

BELOW AND RIGHT
Tryptich of the Last Judgement (details showing beggars with babe in arms and street scene), Barend Van Orley, early 16th century

Life in medieval Glasgow

So what was daily life like before the Industrial Revolution got the wrecker's ball swinging? How did the people of Glasgow live when the Molendinar burn still flowed above ground, when Provand's Lordship was but one of over thirty imposing stone built manses, clustered around the cathedral, or when the university was getting going on the High Street?

A reliable sense of the layout of the medieval burgh can yet be gleaned from John Slezer's engravings, published in the sixteen nineties, which depict the cathedral and the college surrounded by open space. By the end of the fifteenth century these two landmarks and trade around the cross provided the focus and locus for most activity in the medieval metropolis. Half a century or so before the changes ushered in by the Reformation, Glasgow was in the grip of one of its periodic fits of energy and self confidence, a 'Miles Better' moment.

Arriving in the Glasgow of just before the year 1500 it's the smell that hits you first, a putrid, pungent, pong. Mingled with the stink of human and animal waste is the acrid stench of the, by now, well established tanneries and the malty musk of the Wellpark Brewery.

It's noisy too, though just outside the city is to be found a rural quiet. Before light pollution what bright noiseless wonder there was on a clear starry night. However by day the hub of medieval Glasgow was alive with the clang and the clatter of a town with wares to buy and sell, vendors loudly proclaiming the quality of their salted salmon, herring, meat, meal and oysters, cloth both fine and functional. Merchants and customers haggling and comparing local and imported goods. Pedlars bang their pans and barrows, literally, to 'drum up' business.

The town is crowded and more than merely goods are traded. Mendicants, wandering friars, beg and preach. Horses clop and whinney. Wagons creak and rattle. Boys from the grammar school joke and jostle. College students quote and quibble on their way to a memory dimming cup of ale. Now that the cathedral has lost its monopoly on worship many church bells ring. Drovers bring cattle and thirsts from Argyll, taking back with them trade items to make rural eyes widen.

Traffic over the old bridge, of eight stone spans, at the Bridgegate, creates congestion on what will become Stockwell Street. That said, most travellers, to and fro, splashed through the calf high water at the famous ford which first drew settlers to the 'Green Hollow'. Indeed this crossing, with its extensive marshlands, some yards to the east of the stone bridge, was still the major means of crossing until the 1770s. But Glasgow is proud of its innovative bridge. One quarry which may have provided the stone for the bridge is on the hill on which the necropolis will later stand. Hammer and chisel and the screams of the maimed will have contributed their ringing top notes to the

35 Terry Jones, *Medieval Lives* (London, 2003)

cacophony. Though the dead leave quietly enough, there is plenty of noise and bustle in and around the city's hospitals.

Distinguishable in robes of black and brown respectively, the Dominican and Franciscan friars have taken no vow of silence as they dispute this or that gloss of Duns Scotus or Aquinas or the merits of Sunday afternoon's soup in the refectory. To the Dominicans is owed Glasgow's university and to this day, the visitor can find freshly made broth, lively conversation and, of course, good ale in the taverns around Blackfriars Street.

In the mid fifteenth century, Glasgow's East End – as we now construe it – had a pronounced votive dimension. The upper town centered around the cathedral while the lower town, is bounded by the confluence of the Clyde and the Molendinar burn and the larger waterway's banks. In 1450 Glasgow Green was effectively designated Britain's first public park, part of the grant of land from King James II (1437-1460) to William Turnbull, Bishop of Glasgow. The town also hosted a weekly market and an annual fair. All human life, as the saying goes, was there.

Yet all of Glasgow's throng, all the sounds and smells, are being made by fewer than two thousand souls. Even by the mid-sixteenth century, the entire population of the city was only equivalent to around four thousand, the average turnout for a Partick Thistle home game.

From the granting of its Papal bull, in 1451, the university, initially using the Dominican's premises could, on the model of Europe's earliest university, Bologna, offer all the subjects of the day: the trivium and quadrivium. In securing a university, Glasgow had scored over its great rival, Dumbarton.

Benefiting from the Clyde's depth and breadth downriver Dumbarton could allow ships to berth. It was not until the establishment, in the seventeenth century, of Port Glasgow, ten miles downstream and provokingly opposite Dumbarton, that Glasgow had a similar capability. For much of the middle ages Glasgow made the best of things attracting, by its prestige and prosperity, goods from farther and farther afield. Broad bottomed, barge-like boats, could navigate the upper reaches of the river, although quays and docks such as Yorkhill and the Broomielaw were a long way off in the future.

The most significant site in Slezer's panoramic prints was, of course the cathedral. Glasgow's first cathedral was grievously damaged by that vexing commonplace of the epoch, a fire, in 1189. The successor to that building's successor was much bigger than ever. Loans from Florentine bankers had helped to fund diocesan and municipal ambition. For all its ecclesiastical pomp and pretension, Glasgow was a relatively poor city in this period. By comparison with other Scottish cities and certainly by the standard of English and many continental cities, Glasgow's economy was fragile. Aberdeen was more economically vibrant.

However by the late fifteenth century, our snapshot moment, wooden shacks and flimsy peasant huts were giving way to more solidly contructed stone dwellings. Many of these, in the upper town at least, were, like Provand's Lordship, substantial. Recent research suggests that, in the late middle ages, the dwellings of the poor were not necessarily poor dwellings. Projecting the notion of the 'shanty town' backwards is misleading. The roofs over medieval heads had to be as resistant to rain as ours. Glasgow's climate was never a dry one.

By the end of the middle ages Glasgow's two principal districts, the upper and lower towns, comprised four intersecting thoroughfares. Their layout and character were quite different. In the lower town the market area and the passages off the main thoroughfares were overcrowded, narrow, airless and gloomy, the buildings leaning towards each other at the top. The upper town was more spacious with large dwellings among gardens and orchards.

A further bit of imaginative time travel brings us to Glasgow Cross formed by the High Street, Trongate, Saltmarket and Gallowgate. About to pass each other, at the crossroads, are four people, who, despite the city's compactness, have never met. They also prove that our medieval forebears were not merely cogs in the collective machine but people, very much alive and very much like us.

The canon's tale

HUGH, A CANON OF THE CATHEDRAL, is a man in his, busy, self assured, ambitious early thirties. He is going places, in more than one sense of the phrase, making his way from Blackfriars, where he has been giving an informal university tutorial on some controversial aspects of Aristotle's ethics. His morning beer and porridge are a distant memory – he was up, as usual, at five – and afternoon dinner is badly wanted, a stew of vegetables and, with luck, a bit of roast meat.

Hugh's diet is a more fortunate one than the fare of many of his contemporaries. Not for him the maddening itches and twitches of Saint Elmo's Fire, a malady brought on by rotten rye bread. Hugh is lucky indeed to only have heard of such horrors from the hospitaler. Upon the cathedral bread one can always depend; on the ale too, and both plentiful. No need to fret over the disease spreading water supply when the beer jugs going round. Ale meant no ailment!

Yet before the first, hoppy, draught of the day, Hugh has the office to say, the round of daily personal prayer that is his defining duty. His vocation is genuine and for him his Christian observance is a source of more pleasure than even a leg of lamb or a drop of beer. Around the Dominicans, who rehearse and revise and re-polish their sermons and lectures, one must always remain on one's mettle. As Hugh has seen, no-one could accuse the Blackfriars of not practising what they preach! Today he feels he could have out-doctored any Dominican. But, as he reminds himself, pride is a sin so he tries to put the thought out of his head.

A keen musician, Hugh's head is full of sacred song. He is entering his lusty prime so some of his songs are not so sacred. As he swishes, cassock aswirl, up the High Street towards the cathedral he, almost literally, bumps into three of his students, intending clerics all. Once young scholars might have risked a ribbing or worse from passers by, less pious than they. However,

ABOVE
Grammar school class

LEFT
A mendicant friar

RIGHT
Medieval maid

BELOW
Carving, Blacader Aisle, Glasgow Cathedral

OPPOSITE
Street market

much of the 'town and gown' tension caused by this determinedly, non-, even anti-secular seat of learning, has begun to die down.

The demeanour of Hugh's students mixes admiration with just a wee bit of cocky combativeness. Since, at least officially, even conversation outwith the lecture room, ought to be in Latin, their teasing witticisms are in the universal language of prayer and scholarship of the day. Greetings are exchanged, again, in Glasgow-accented Latin.

The book one of the students is carrying is a masterwork, nearly nine hundred years old. Boethius, *On The Consolations of Philosophy*, has, like all books of the time, been copied out by hand. Seeing it reminds Hugh that, for his early evening class, he must remember his copy of a treatise on Gratian's *Decretum*, a founding text of church jurisprudence written in 1140. The book is in his lodgings, very conveniently situated on Drygate in one of the manses, much like the building in Castle Street which one day will be restyled 'Provand's Lordship'. Hugh's riposte elicits giggles, handshakes and a little (well concealed) hero worship – well not precisely worship, given the context and the ubiquity of God in medieval Europe.

The mason's tale

Watching the purposeful priest head hurriedly uphill, is a worn and weary looking man, old for the times, at fifty or so. Having crossed the sturdy bridge from the south he has travelled, along from the Trongate, and arrived at the junction. Peter hirples, he is, 'shilpit'. Many years ago a bulky block of stone, viciously tumbling, broke the mason's back as he carved, at ground level. His own task had been the intricate cutting of blonde facing stones. That had been in his youth, so far behind him now that it hardly seems his at all. That distant boyhood seems so detached from his experience and recall.

Mind you Peter had toiled on as a stonemason. He had begun his working life as a quarryman, paid for whatever weight he could hew, as a pieceworker. But after a hard apprenticeship his 'craft', earned him the right to seek employment where he had a notion to. He was indeed a free mason. And the guilds had won payment by the hour, not the amount of labour. 'Lame Pedie' had even prospered. His guild had paid his hospital bills and lost wages, lobbying as he recuperated, for greater care to be taken on building sites.

The young scholars banter on in Latin. Whatever is written in their books, will forever be a puzzle to Peter. He lets out a wheezy breath, recalling old wounds and worries. Were he a lad again, he'd look to his learning and letters. But with no such knowledge he'd be unable to make out even his own name on his headstone. Soon with a bit of help, he'll carve it all the same. In France, he has heard, one master builder signed a cathedral, 'Gislebertus Hoc Fecit'. Sadly he has nowhere quite so grand upon which to carve 'Peter made this!'

It is Peter's meal break, the slightly longer lunch-hour of one pitied and respected, and he has a fresh young salmon, procured near the bridge. Peter's hometown of Glasgow is not too far removed from a fishing village at this time. In its Fishergate and down by the river itself, there will have been gossip to catch as well as salmon and trout. There are farm and fishing communities just beyond the city's gates, or 'ports' and news is handed over with the tolls as visitors seek to sell and buy.

Peter notices a pretty girl browsing by the goldsmiths, trying on a bracelet, sees the priest professor noticing her too. Peter sighs. His good wife is long dead. She died giving birth to a darling daughter, about that girl's age, if she had lived. If Margaret had only lived. Just two of the nine bairns she bore survived. One of those daughters will poach the salmon. Another will set out the board. The thought of his daughters lifts Peter's heart as he heads homeward.

The maid's tale

Our third traveller, Anna, arrives from Saltmarket. There, her employer, a minor but moneyed noble, maintains a large and impressive family residence. Anna is abroad on his wife's behalf. At her behest this young fifteenth century Glaswegian is glad to be out on the prowl. Most of the household's needs are met by provisions delivered to the (back) door. But the morning markets must be scowered for the choicest cheeses, finest fruits, freshest fish and the most mouth watering meat.

Anna harbours a secret, she may be out on her mistress's business but this little shopping expedition is also for Anna herself. Not given to frippery or extravagance, she is this winter afternoon, well wrapped in heat retaining, hodden grey, a blankety shawl, neither brown nor grey nor beige. Her outfit is warm, if unbecoming. Even in her finest garb, the maidservant cannot compete with her mistress. In the later middle ages, manners maketh man but, as her ladyship's husband quips, 'garments make the woman'!

Anna's best outfit is reserved for church, a long dress with fashionable, 'continental' slashes and ribbons wound round her brooches. Her embroidered 'Sunday' bonnet was made and bought to attract attention. As of last Sunday, and a fateful walk after morning mass, Anna is all but betrothed to a comely young fellow whose eye she has spent a conniving half-year trying to catch.

She has decided that a bonny new shawl should seal her matrimonial bargain. On the alibi of being out to purchase kale that is what she is truly after, yellow for preference, saffron silk. Or a blithe, blameless blue. The dyes for those are easily got, garments in either shade readily affordable, even for young girls in the pay of miserly masters. Her mistress can order far more costly clothes in Anna's favourite colour, bright, blazing red, rarest of all the far travelled hues of the age.

Anna is not to know, that afternoon, where four Glasgow streets converge, that in one of the most touching letters to survive from that age, a lady, Mistress Paston, not unlike her own, unperturbable, mistress wrote to her absent spouse, that she would sooner have him safely home than even a dress of scarlet. What a happy and alas, atypical, lovematch that was.

Of course people in the middle ages did, on occasion, marry out of longing and loyalty but more often for those with wealth or position, parental pressure, economic necessity or dynastic advance was the cause. Anna, poor and with no such pressures, has a reasonable chance of contentment. That is if plague, famine, fire or flood don't make off with one or other of the happy couple. Profit, politics and power made a bride of the grand lady in whose service Anna labours. A marriage of kin and convenience, tepid, certainly, but not without its solaces and civilities and the occasional love-cry in the night.

Blue, Anna thinks, blue to match her eyes. She overhears the handsome canon, quipping with his pupils, in a tongue she knows only a smattering of from her punctual and pious attendance at the Church of St Thomas. He is, she admits, even better looking than her beau. As many young serving girls have cause to know, chastity is, for a good number of priests with roving eyes, the most abstract of vows. A song of the time described the attitude of many friars,

"Down the broad way I go,
Young and unregretting,
Wrap me in my vices,
Virtue all forgetting."[36]

Anna's young master, the son and heir, though a student of theology himself, has commented often since reaching puberty on the blue of the young servant's eyes. She has been lucky to ward off his advances because women of the time are often subject to the unwelcome attentions of men of money or power. A contemporary poem gives some impression of the position of women in the middle ages,

"A woman is a worthy wight,
She serveth both by day and night,
Thereto she putteth all her might,
And yet she hath but care and woe".[37]

Many of the alehouses of the period were however run by women, often widows, and there were female barbour surgeons and doctors. Most women however were denied education, penalised by inheritance law, kept in their place by self perpetuating male dominance. Women, whether served or serving, didn't have an easy time of it. If a cloak of gold could help then it should. Her thoughts now turning to the matter of her dowry kist, young Anna walks on.

The apothecary's tale

ARMS FLAILING, HAIR BLOWING in the wind, running down the Gallowgate, William has no time to observe, Hugh, Peter or Anna. He is oblivious, impervious, unreachable. He has just delivered opiates to the woman caring for a dying man across from the cathedral, without telling his employer. So Willie is now late for work, very late, again. He is on the way to the apothecary's shop where he is apprenticed in the healing arts of herbalism, potion and tincture mixing and the dispensing of remedies and cures.

William and his master are proud of their professionalism. William is irked by the mountebanks and 'snake-oil' salesmen who peddle their pills and panaceas on Glasgow Green. Although like many of his contemporaries Willie believes in relics, miracles and apparitions he is scientist enough to know that the pseudo physicians of the market and the annual fair belong with the jugglers, ballad hawkers and fire-eaters. These imposters manage through their persuasive patter. As the would be apothecary knows, Salerno, is the pre-eminent centre of medical knowledge of the age, blessed as it is by Islamic learning.

Willie recalls the popular prescription "First do no harm, then, use three physicians' skill, first, Dr Quiet, next Dr Merryman and third, Dr Diet!" The influential Arab surgeon, Constantius, was wise indeed. We now know that many of the 'primitive' treatments of the time were truly effective. Leeches, for instance, are now farmed, such is their effectiveness in cleaning wounds. They even come complete with their own anaesthetic, dispensed by means of their saliva. In William's day, leeching is barbers' work.

The monks of the age look after themselves. In every monastic community one of the brothers ministers to the mortally ill. They are expert in the signs of impending death, judging, almost to the second, from fading pulse, shortening breath and darkening urine, when the spirit is ready to be given up. William's own master had studied with an old Franciscan.

On a normal day, when not in a rush, Willie would stare longingly at the newest, most elegant saddles on the saddler's tressle. But before acquiring a saddle he would have to acquire a mount and, indeed, learn to ride for that matter. Poorly paid Willie is only in learning his trade. The would-be pharmacist must wait until he can afford to put a saddle before the horse.

As he runs on, Willie has no time to collect the boots he has left for repair. The 'good' shoes he is wearing oughtn't to be exposed to the slime and slither of the winter streets. As he skitters past Anna, very nearly slipping to the ground, he registers the blue of her eyes, with a pang.

Turning into Trongate, Willie sees his master in the middle distance, thick arms folded, exasperatedly impatient, no indulgent smile today. The boy is too preoccupied to take in the slow, stiff progress of the ancient stonemason, Peter. Liquors from the present pharmacist's father eased Peter's wife's passage from the world. The same pestle and mortar had ground the powder that soothed the stonemason's own pain after his accident.

Our fifteenth century foursome are all unique individuals. In the rich pageant of Glasgow's history, each is special, a one-off. The church of the

36 M Rowling, *Life in Medieval Times* (New York, 1968) 37 P J P Goldberg (ed.), *Women in Medieval English Society c. 1200-1500* (Shroud, 1997)

BELOW AND RIGHT
Tryptich of the Last Judgement (details showing death bed and burial – with momenti mori), Barent Van Orley, early 16th century

OPPOSITE
Medieval pilgrims

OVERLEAF
Pages from manuscript of Kentigern: De Vita Sua by Jocelin of Furness, 12th century

time was undoubtedly powerful. Our four citizens knew their place in the hierarchical scheme of things. Life was a struggle but it was also precious. All educated Glaswegians of the time knew that the earth wasn't flat. They knew that the mythical creatures carrying their heads under their arms on the 'mappa mundae' were just that. These fanciful creatures were merely abstract perils in distant lands. But our four, on this particular day, are preoccupied by the much more immediate realities of day-to-day life in thriving medieval Glasgow.

The ancient's tale

NEAR THE OTHER CROSSROADS of the fifteenth century city, in the upper town, across from Rottenrow, in a rather woebegone wooden dwelling, two old men are talking in low, quivering voices. Their mood is mournful and melancholy, striving now and then for a note of defiant gaiety. At almost eighty, this pair really are old, practically biblical. One of them is propped up in bed, a fur cloak thrown over the covers to keep out the cold and damp. He has perhaps a week to live, and he knows it. No-one this old has avoided brushes with mortality.

He is composed and ready, whether for heaven, hell, or oblivion. In the midst of life, death; in the midst of faith, doubt. This afternoon, he rather thinks it will be a dreamless doze among the maggots. By this evening, in his fever, he may hope again for an afterlife not unlike that promised by the preachers in the cathedral and the reassuring wood carvings and colourful stained glass behind them.

God is ever present in the life of the city, an overlord, mightier than any feudal strongman, capable of intervening, for good or ill, in one's daily doings, turning troubles into triumphs or vice versa.

A longtime scoffer, now that his end is finally nigh, the invalid is at last in doubt. Amidst groans and grimaces, he will soon perish. Now he doesn't know what he believes or believe what he knows. In fine French wine, he has inveterately had faith. This afternoon however, he has neither the strength nor the palate for even a sip from the flagon of Bordeaux his old friend has brought for their mutual consolation.

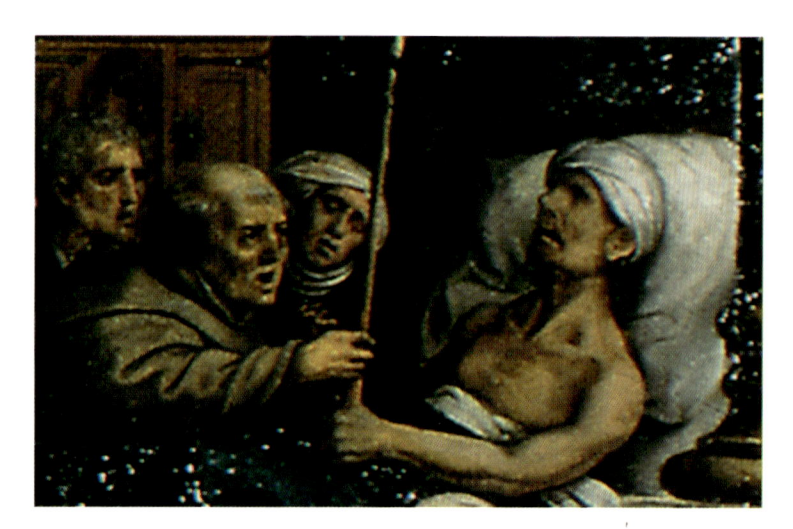

The watcher by the deathbed is called Gillespie. He wonders, as his comrade sleeps and from time to time feebly rallies, how and when he himself will breathe his last. It is his expensive sable cloak spread upon the blankets, a souvenir of happier, healthy and flusher times. He bought it in Paris, at the fair of L'endit or St Denis, with money won at dice.

The two first met at the Sorbonne. The university of Glasgow had not yet been founded, wouldn't exist until 1451, so Gillespie had studied at Balliol, the Oxford college associated with Scotland. From there he headed to Paris. As a private scholar and tutor, Gillespie had done stints at Padua and Heidelberg, going on to help found Glasgow's own university in due course. Originally a man of Argyll, he has also visited Ireland.

Gillespie's great, great grandfather would scarcely have distinguished between the Gaeltachts of Ireland and Scotland, Eire and Alba. But the idea of 'Scotland' had been forged in law and lore, in the library and on the battlefield. Scotland was Gillespie's country and Glasgow his city. As tutor to one of the older Scottish lineages, Gillespie has skirmished in their cause. A deep cleft in his shoulder, which had never properly healed and the stiffness that went with it, thankfully not in his writing and sword wielding arm, were Gillespie's mementos of that affiliation.

There was a scar too, across Gillespies' brow and bracketing his left eye. Sight in that eye had been impaired. Skilled barber surgeons had saved the eye. For a while Gillespie had sported a kidskin patch with such dash and glamour that he had been almost sorry when it was no longer needed, as indeed, had more than one neglected gudwife.

Fortunately for the sake of his companion, Gillespie's passion for the woman who owned this alehouse and its lodgings had cooled more quickly than her widow's heart. Gillespie lived nearby. Often in the wee hours he would awaken, trapped once more in battle, amid a clashing forest of steel, his own screams and warcries mingling with the martial din. In another frequent nightmare, he is back hiding in a ditch, waiting for the 'finisher off' who never came, or passed on, leaving the badly wounded and the unconscious Gillespie for dead.

Smiling sadly while mopping his friend's scorching forehead, he knows he has lived too long, outlasting fortune, fate and all but one contemporary. Our apothecary's friend William would have coveted his boots, strong and supple, Cordova's finest. For Hugh, the teacher priest, what fascination there would have been in the book Gillespie had pressed upon his friend, once such a greedy reader, an illustrated edition of Chaucer, beautifully bound, now, like the wine, rejected. His Arras shirt and frayed but exquisite crimson tunic, woven bargained for and bought in Ghent, would have impressed the maid

Anna, as would the brooch of Norwegian silver that gathered it. Peter, the ancient stonemason, would have acknowledged Gillespie as a kindred spirit.

Gillespie came close to envying outright his stricken friend's acceptance of his fate. A hundred years; two hundred years, wouldn't be life enough for him. For the printing presses he had heard about, he had to live! For the new learning! From the chatter of churchmen and scholars, he knew about the latest scientific speculations, knew too of dissatisfaction with the Pope and how it meshed with the rise of princes and the burgesses. For all that he had to live! Had to!

Independence of mind and spirit, a fondness for the Scots vernacular, a mistrust of ceremony and solemnity, impatience with ecclesiastical politics, a yen for more and better schools, these traits would have made Gillespie a sincere and energetic Protestant. But the Reformation of Calvin, Melville and Knox is several decades away and in a while, all too wee a while, the will to live must give way, even for Gillespie, to the last will and testament.

Gillespie fidgets with the ring he wears on his little finger, loosening it by degrees, like his friend's grip on life. The candlelight is coming and going with the glow flickering fitfully in the resting patient's, half open, green eyes. Draining his goblet and with a wistful squeeze of the hand for his now peacefully slumbering friend, Gillespie directs a murmured word of thanks to the widow's daughter who cares for the dying man.

The girl is very visibly pregnant. Why didn't Gillespie notice before? There had been a boy of his in Bruges, a son, five years dead, before word had come to Gillespie. The same letter, from his sweetheart's mother, informed him of his lover's demise. With the letter arrived the ring he'd given her, a good ring, a cloudy emerald set in its broad, bright band. Why hadn't they kept it or sold it? And he, as so often, more kissed than kissing, having loved and left, had mattered more to her, than she to he. However for Gillespie she had mattered, truly mattered, every day since.

It used to be thought by historians that 'romantic' love was a literary construct, a fervent fiction of troubadour poetry. Ask Gillespie about that! Ask about April evenings, down by the harbour in Bruges. Love was as true in Gillespie's time as it is, in our own. It is true too, then as now, that young women who are with child palpably bloom.

Brooding on the hopes and hazards of that condition and on loves and losses of his own, the old man heads down the High Street. He heads for home through the stink and clamour, the life affirming noise and noxiousness. Gillespie is happy in spite of it all, smiling, glad to be, wine warmed, above ground, truly alive. And he heads out of sight, lost, in what, his prodigious learning notwithstanding, he cannot know, historians will one day call, "medieval Glasgow".

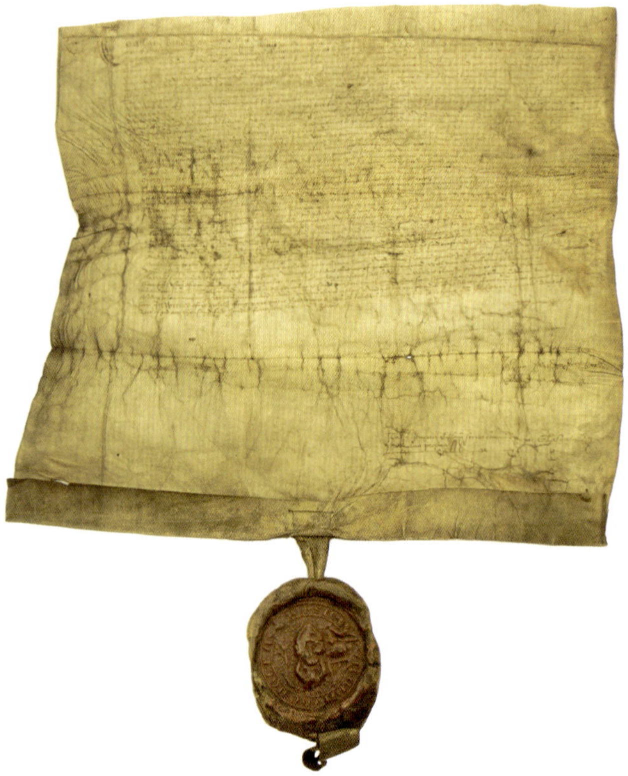

Bibliography

Primary sources and reference works

J. Bain and C. Rogers (eds) *The Protocol Book of Cuthbert Simon 1499-1513* (Grampian Club, 1875)

P. Hume Brown (ed.) *Early Travellers in Scotland* (Edinburgh, 1891)

N.M de S. Cameron, D.F. Wright and D.C. Lachman (eds), *Dictionary of Scottish Church History and Theology* (Edinburgh, 1993)

Charters and Documents of Glasgow (British History Online, Institute of Historical Research, University of London) www.british-history.ac.uk

Charters and other Documents relating to the City of Glasgow (Scottish Burgh Records Soc., 1894-1906)

I.B. Cowan and D.E. Easson (eds) *Medieval Religious Houses: Scotland* (London, 1976)

W.C. Dickinson, *The Barony Court Book of Carnwath, 1523-1542* (Edinburgh, 1937)

W.C. Dickinson (ed.) *Early Records of the Burgh of Aberdeen* (Edinburgh, 1957)

W.C. Dickinson (ed.) *The Sheriff Court Book of Fife, 1515-1522* (Edinburgh, 1928)

Robert Henryson, G.D. Gopen (ed.) *The Morall Fabillis of Esope the Phrygian* (Edinburgh, 1987)

J. Kirk (ed.) *Scottish Ecclesiastical Rentals at the Reformation* (Oxford, 1995)

Sir David Lindsay of the Mount, R. Lyall (ed.) *Ane Satyre of the Thrie Estaitis* (Edinburgh, 1989)

J.D Marwick (ed.) *Extracts from the Records of the Burgh of Glasgow* (Glasgow, 1876)

P.G.B. McNeill (ed.) *Discours Particulier D'Escosse* in D.H. Sellar (ed.), *Stair Miscellany II* (Edinburgh, 1984)

P.G.B. McNeill and H.L. MacQueen (eds) *Atlas of Scottish History to 1707* (Edinburgh, 1996)

Origines Parochiales Scotiae (Bannatyne Club, 1851)

R. Pitcairn (ed.) *Criminal Trials in Scotland from 1488 to 1624*, 3 vols (Edinburgh, 1833)

Registrum Episcopatus Glasguensis (Bannatyne and Maitland Clubs, 1843)

The Rental Book of the Diocese of Glasgow (Grampian Club, 1875)

R. Renwick (ed.) *Abstracts of the Protocols of the Town Clerks of Glasgow, 1547-1600* (Glasgow, 1894-1900)

T. Thomson and C, Innes (eds) *Acts of the Parliaments of Scotland* (Edinburgh, 1814-75)

Secondary sources: books

A.D.M Barrell, *Medieval Scotland* (Cambridge, 2000)

G.W.S. Barrow, *Robert Bruce* (Edinburgh, 1982)

G.W.S. Barrow, *Kingship and Unity: Scotland 1000-1306* (London, 1981)

N. Baxter, *The Wee Green Book* (Glasgow, 2007)

A.L. Brown and M. Moss, *The University of Glasgow: 1451-2001* (Edinburgh, 2001)

J.T.T. Brown, *The Inquest of David* (Glasgow, 1901)

T.M. Cooper, *The Dark Age of Scottish Legal History, 1350-1650* (Edinburgh, 1957)

I.B. Cowan, *The Medieval Church in Scotland* (Edinburgh, 1995)

J. Darragh, *History of the Province of Glasgow* (Western Catholic Calendar, 1990)

E.P. Dennison, D. Ditchburn and M. Lynch (eds) *Aberdeen Before 1800. A New History* (East Linton, 2002)

S.T. Driscoll, *Alba: The Gaelic Kingdom of Scotland, AD 800-1124* (Edinburgh, 2002)

S.T. Driscoll, *Excavations at Glasgow Cathedral, 1988-1997* (Leeds, 2002)

A.A.M. Duncan, *Scotland: The Making of the Kingdom* (Edinburgh, 1978)

J. Durkan, *The Precinct of Glasgow Cathedral* (Glasgow, 1986)

J. Durkan, *William Turnbull, Bishop of Glasgow* (1951)

E. Ewan, *Townlife in Fourteenth-Century Scotland* (Edinburgh, 1990)

G. Eyre-Todd (ed.) *The Book of Glasgow Cathedral: A History and Description* (Glasgow, 1898)

R. Fawcett, *Glasgow Cathedral* (Edinburgh, 1985)

R. Fawcett (ed.) *Medieval Art and Architecture in the Diocese of Glasgow* (Leeds, 1998)

R. Fawcett, *Scottish Abbeys and Priories* (London, 1994)

R. Fawcett, *Scottish Cathedrals* (London, 1997)

R. Fawcett, *Scottish Medieval Churches: Architecture and Furnishings* (Stroud, 2002)

A. Gibb, *Glasgow: The Making of a City* (London, 1983)

J. Gibson, *The History of Glasgow from the Earliest Accounts to the Present Time* (Glasgow, 1777)

J. Gillingham and R. Griffiths, *Medieval Britain, a Very Short Introduction* (Oxford, 1984)

P.J.P Goldberg (ed.) *Woman in Medieval English Society c. 1200-1500* (Stroud, 1997)

T. Jones, *Medieval Lives* (London, 2003)

M. Lynch, M. Spearman and G. Stell (eds) *The Scottish Medieval Town* (Edinburgh, 1988)

J. Macaulay, *The Western Towers of Glasgow Cathedral* (Glasgow, 1998)

L.J. Macfarlane, *William Elphinstone and the Kingdom of Scotland, 1431-1514* (Aberdeen, 1985)

A. MacGeorge, *Old Glasgow, the Place and the People* (3rd edn, London, 1888)

J. Mackay, *Pocket Scottish History* (Glasgow, 2006)

A. McColl, *The Medieval Underworld* (London, 1979)

J.A. McUre, *View of the City of Glasgow* (Glasgow, 1736)

A.H. Millar, *Bygone Glasgow* (Glasgow, 1896)

D. Murray, *Early Burgh Organisation in Scotland, vol. 1, Glasgow* (Glasgow, 1924)

D. Murray, *Memories of the Old College of Glasgow* (Glasgow, 1927)

P. Reed, *Glasgow, the Forming of the City* (Edinburgh, 1999)

R. Reid (Senex), *Glasgow Past and Present* (Glasgow, 1884)

R. Renwick, *Glasgow Memorials* (Glasgow, 1908)

R. Renwick, *The Archepiscopal Temporalities in the Regality of Glasgow* (Glasgow, 1905)

R. Renwick and J. Lindsay, *History of Glasgow Vol.1 Pre-Reformation Period* (Glasgow, 1921)

M. Rowling, *Life in Medieval Times* (New York, 1968)

M.H.B. Sanderson, 'Mark Ker 1517-1584: metamorphosis' in M.H.B. Sanderson, *Mary Stewart's People* (Edinburgh, 1987)

A.P. Smyth, *Warlords and Holy Men* (Edinburgh, 1994)

F. Watson, *Scotland from the Prehistory to the Present* (Stroud, 2001)

B. Webster, *Medieval Scotland, the Making of Identity* (London, 1997)

J. Wormold, *Court, Kirk and Community* (Edinburgh, 1981)

Secondary sources: articles and other material

G. Chambers, 'Provand's Lordship', Glasgow Archaeological Soc. Bulletin, new series 4, no. 1 (1977)

I.B. Cowan, 'The emergence of the urban parish', in M. Lynch, M. Spearman and G. Stell (eds) *The Scottish Medieval Town* (Edinburgh, 1988)

I.B. Cowan, 'Glasgow Cathedral and its clergy in the middle ages', *Annual Report of the Society of Friends of Glasgow Cathedral* (1976)

M. Cross, *Land Use and Ownership History of the Greyfriars Site in Glasgow* (Headland Archaeology, Nov. 2005)

T.A. Davidson Kelly, *The Prebend of Govan, 1150-1560* from www.govanold.org.uk

S.T. Driscoll, 'Church archaeology in Glasgow and the kingdom of Strathclyde', *Innes Review*, 49, no. 2 (Autumn, 1998)

J. Durkan, 'Cadder and environs and the development of the church in Glasgow in the twelfth century', *Innes Review*, 49, no. 2 (Autumn, 1998)

J. Durkan, 'Care of the poor, pre-Reformation hospitals', *Innes Review*, 10 (1959)

J. Durkan, 'The bishop's barony of Glasgow in pre-Reformation times', *Records of the Scottish Church History Society*, 22 (1984-86)

'Glasgow Aquinas Lecture' delivered by Rev. Allan White OP in the Bute Hall as part of Glasgow University's 550th Jubilee

Glasgow Provosts (Glasgow City Archive AGN1541)

J.R. Kellett, 'Glasgow' in M.D. Lobel (ed.) *Historic Towns*, vol. 1 (London, 1969)

L.J. Macfarlane, 'The elevation of the diocese of Glasgow into an archbishopric in 1492', *Innes Review*, 43, no. 2 (Autumn, 1992)

T.M. Devine and G. Jackson (eds) *Glasgow, vol. 1. Beginnings to 1830* (Manchester, 1995)

J. McGrath, *Neighbourhoods, the Regality*, from www.theglasgowstory.com

D. McKay, 'The duties of the medieval parish clerk', *Innes Review*, 19, no. 1 (Spring, 1968)

D. McKay, 'The election of parish clerks in medieval Scotland', *Innes Review*, 18, no. 1 (Spring, 1967)

D. McKay, 'The induction of the parish clerk in medieval Scotland', *Innes Review*, 20, no.1 (Spring, 1969)

I. Maver, *Neighbourhoods, The Barony*, from www.theglasgowstory.com

D.H. Sellar, *Farewell to Feudalism*, from Burke's Peerage and Gentry www.burkes-peerage.net

N. Shead, 'Glasgow: an ecclesiastical burgh', in M. Lynch, M. Spearman and G. Stell (eds) *The Scottish Medieval Town* (Edinburgh, 1988)

N. Shead, 'The origins of the medieval diocese of Glasgow', *Scottish Historical Review*, 48 (1969)

N. Shead, Review of S.T. Driscoll, *Excavations at Glasgow Cathedral 1988-1997*, *Innes Review*, 54, no.2 (Autumn, 2003)

Society of Friends of Glasgow Cathedral, *Annual Report 1967*

E.L.G. Stones, 'Notes on Glasgow Cathedral, the burials of medieval Scottish bishops with particular reference to the bishops of Glasgow', *Innes Review*, 20, no.1 (Spring, 1969)

Glossary

Appropriation	process of diverting parish income to another individual or institution
Apsidal	domed or vaulted multi-sided or semi-circular building, often part of a church
Bellcote	structure on top of a roof housing a bell or bells
Burgage	the tenure of burgh land direct from the Crown
Burgage plot	a piece of land allocated to a burgess
Burgess	a person enjoying the privilege of freedom of a burgh
Choir	(architectural) part of a church in front of the altar lined on both sides by benches and used by the choir and clergy
Conventual	of or relating to a convent or friary
Entrepôt	market centre or port through which trade passes
Fore	set in front
Fulling mill	a mill for beating or cleaning cloth using soap or fuller's earth
Hermitage	the abode of a hermit
Minster	a large church which supplied clergy to surrounding churches
Motte	a natural or man-made mound on which a castle was built
Office	(religious) set of prayers or hymns
Possessory	(legal term) relating to possession
Prebend	source of financial support to a canon or member of a cathedral or collegiate church
Rath	a hill, mound or circular fortified enclosure
Suffragan	bishop or diocese subordinate to and assisting an archbishop or archdiocese
Teind	tithe or payments derived from the produce of the land for the maintenance of parish clergy
Toft	a burgage plot
Toun	a settlement
Waulk mill	another term for fulling mill

Glasgow Cathedral, west window, Creation *by Francis Spear, 1958*

Index

A

Aberdeen 11, 14-16, 18, 58-61, 65, 66, 73, 79
Aberdeen, bishop of 34
Aberdeen Tolbooth 59
Aberdeen University 34
Albion Street 13, 60
Alexander I 22, 24
Alexander II 27, 28
Alexander III 24, 26, 28, 49
Ancrum 41
Angles 22
Anglo-Saxon 22
Annandale 40
Anne, St 19
Aquinas 78
Archbishop 45
archbishop, Protestant 16
Archbishop Beaton's tower 63
Archbishop Dunbar's gateway 63
archbishopric 18
archdeacon 25, 26
archdeaconry 26
Argyll 22, 24, 28, 61, 78, 82
Aristotle 79
Arran, earl of 27
arthritis 73
Ashkirk 28
Askirk 41
Auchinairn 42
Aula, Thomas de 36
Auld Pedagogy 18, 52, 61
Auxerre 24
Ayr 27, 32, 33, 34, 36
Ayrshire 13, 22, 23, 25

B

Badermonoc 41, 42
bailie(s) 42
bakers 15, 50, 72
Balfour, James 33
Balfours Practicks 33
Ballain 41
Balliol 82
Balliol, Edward 27
Balornock 42
Bamburgh 22
Banffshire 65
Bannatyne, William 33
Baptist, St John the 51
Bar-lenerk *see Barlanark*
Bardi 28
Barlanark 41-43, 45
Barlannerc 42
Barmulloch 42
barony 10, 11
Barrasyett 51
baxters 15, 72
Beaton, Archbishop James (I) 27, 63
Beaton, Archbishop James (II) 16, 27, 45, 66
Becket, Archbishop Thomas 52
Becket, St Thomas 25
Bedlay 41
Beg, Malcolm 34
Beith 23
Benedict, St 44
Bergman, Ingmar 78

Bernicia 22
Berwick 40
Birkmyre, Andrew 34
Birrell, Sir Andrew 45
bishop 43
bishop's burgh 10, 14, 15, 16, 18
bishop's castle 11, 13, 15, 51, 62, 63, 74
Bishop's Loch 42
Bishop Bondington 65
bishopric 10, 14, 16
bishops forest 23, 41
Blacader, Archbishop 13, 24, 27, 42, 45, 60, 62, 66
Blacader, Roland 26, 52
Blacader's Hospital 13
Blacader Aisle 15, 66
Blackadder *see Blacader*
Black Death 19, 23, 27
Blackfriars 16, 44, 61, 79
Blackfriars Street 78
Blackness 14, 50, 53
blacksmiths 53
Blairtummock 42
Blessed Virgin 25
Bo'ness 14
Boethius 79
Bologna 79
Bondington, Bishop William de 25, 43
bonnetmakers 15
Bordeaux 82
Border 25
Borders 35
Brereton, William 14

brewing 15
bridge 11, 13, 15, 19, 26, 45, 52, 73, 78
Bridgegate 16, 49, 51, 54, 78
Bridgegate Port 51
Brigend 36
British Isles 65
Britons 32
Broomielaw 79
Bruce 40
Bruce, Robert 26, 32
bubonic 73
Budlornac 42
bull(s) 10, 11, 28, 36, 44, 49, 61, 79
Bun's Wynd 51
burgess(es) 14, 15, 19
burgh 10, 11, 14, 18
burgh market 51
burn 13
butchers 50, 72

C

Cadfael 78
Cadzow 42
Cambridge 78
Cambridge Street 35
Cameron, Bishop John 25, 43, 61, 66
Camlachie Burn 16, 49, 51
Candleriggs 53, 54, 71
canons 13, 43
canons' dwellings 13, 15
Canterbury 52
Canterbury, archbishop of 24
Carham 22
Carham, battle of 22

caries 73
Carlisle 24, 26
Carmyle 42
carpenters 13
Carrick, dean of 33
Carstairis *see Carstairs*
Carstairs 41
Carver, Robert 78
castle 13, 51, 63
Castle Port 51
Castle Street 62
Castleyett 51
cathedral 10, 11, 13, 15, 16, 19, 23-25, 34, 43, 49-51, 58, 61-63, 65, 66, 74, 78, 79, 81
cathedral chapter 34, 43
cathedral choir school 60
Catholic 16, 66
Cathures 22
Catterick 22
chancellor 25, 27, 62
chancellor, Catholic 18
Chanonry 61
chapel 15
chapel of St Roche 19
Chapel Royal 66
chapels 13
chaplains 13
Charles II 16
Cheam, Bishop John de 26, 42
cholera 19, 73
choristers 14
Christ 66
Christian 79
church 13
church, Franciscan 19
church, Scottish 10, 24
Church of St Thomas 80
Cistercian 23
City Improvement Act of 1866 19
City Science 13, 60
civil war 18
Clairvaux 24
Clement VII of Avignon 28
clergy 14
cloth 15
Clyde 11, 15, 23, 28, 33, 49, 50, 52, 53, 58, 62, 63, 70, 73, 78, 79
Coatbridge 42

cobblers 53
Cochmanach 34
Cochno 34
cold, common 73
college 50, 78
College Goods Yard 60
collegiate church 15
Comyn, John 26
Conclud 40, 42
Constantine, St 28
Constantius 81
Convention of Royal Burghs 16
Cooper, Lord President 37
cordiners 15, 50, 72
Corpus Christi 74
council 18
Court of Lords Auditors 27
Cowdenknowes, laird of 33
craftsmen 15
Craig's Park 62
Craignaught 53, 54
cross of Lorraine 16
Cumberland 24
Cumbria 11, 22, 24, 28, 32
Cumbria, Prince of 32, 40
Cumbrian(s) 22
Cumbric 22
Cunningham, dean of 33
Curia, Peter de 27

D
Dalriada 22
David 24, 41
David, Earl 32
David I 22, 23, 26, 28, 34, 41, 43, 51, 65
dean 25, 62
Deanside Well 51
de Brus 40
Decretum 79
Denis, St 82
Denmark 27
Denniston, Charles 32
diocese 10, 11, 15
Dobbies Loan 51, 52
Dominic, St 44
Dominican(s) 13, 26, 44, 50, 52, 59, 74, 78, 79
Dominican chapter house 52
Dominican friary 54

Drumpellier 42
Drygate 16, 50, 51, 53, 62
Drygate Port 51
Dublin 22
Duchal castle 27
Dugald 33
Dumbarton 11, 14, 22, 23, 28, 50, 53, 79
Dumbarton, kingdom of 23
Dumbarton, Royal Burgh of 28
Dumbarton Castle 27
Dumbarton Rock 22, 28
Dumfries and Galloway 49
Dumfries Sheriff Court 32
Dunbar, Archbishop 42, 60, 63
Dunblane 24
Dundee 14, 15, 16
Dunfermline 15
Dunkeld 24
Dunnichen 22
Duns Scotus 78
Durham 10
Durisdeer, Bishop Andrew de 25, 27
dyers 15, 50, 53
dysentry, amoebic 73

E
Eaglesham 62
Easter 35
Easter Commons 42
Easterhouse 45
East Port 51
Eco, Umberto 78
Edgar, King 22
Edinbarnet 34
Edinbernan 34
Edinburgh 11, 14, 16, 22, 50, 53
Edlistoun 41
Edward (son of Malcolm III) 40
Edward I 27, 32, 59, 65
Edward II 27
Edward III 27
Edward the Confessor, St 66
Elgin 60, 66
Elizabeth II 65
Elphinstone, William 34
England 11, 15, 22, 24, 26, 40
English 22, 24, 25, 27, 32, 65
Enlightenment 78

Enoch, St. 10, 52
Epiphany 23
Erskine Bridge 33
Eskil 24
Eugenius III 24
Europe 15, 37, 65, 79
Europe, Western 27, 33

F
Faculty of Arts 52
fair(s) *see also Glasgow Fair* 10, 11, 44, 49, 53, 72, 73, 74, 81
Ferdan, Bede 33, 34
Ferdan, Cristin 34
Fergus of Galloway 23
Fife, sheriff court of 32
fire 19
fire, great 19
Fishergate 50, 53, 80
fishermen 50
Fitzalan 40
Fitzhugh, Alexander 33, 34
fleshers 50, 72
Florentine 28, 79
football 35
Forbes, Sir Thomas 45
ford 11
Forfarshire 28
Forth, River 22
Forth ports 14
Fourth Lateran Council 24, 27
France 16, 80
Francis, St 44
Franciscan(s) 13, 19, 44, 51, 52, 59, 60, 74, 78, 81
Franciscan friary 15, 16, 54
Franciscan Observants 44
free forest 42
French 28, 32, 33, 65, 82
French Revolution 66
friaries 11, 13
Friars Preachers 44
friary church 15
fruit 16
fullers 16
fulling 53
fulling mills 16

G

Galbraith, Alexander 60
Galloway 13, 22, 24, 26
Gallowgate 16, 36, 49, 50, 51-53, 79, 81
Gallowgate Port 51
Gallowmuir 42
gallows 36
Gargunnock 34
Garioch 41, 42
Garngad 53
Gartinqueen 42
Gaskel, Thomas 34
gates 15
General Assembly 16
George Street 13, 60
Gerard of Rome 27
Gilbert 33, 34
Gilbethoc 34
Gilmorehill 52, 60
gingivitis 73
Glasgow Cross 79
Glasgow Fair 10, 43, 44
Glasgow Fort 62
Glasgow Grammar School 60
Glasgow Green 40, 53, 79, 81
Glasgow High School 61
Glasgow Sheriff Court 32, 35
Glasgow University 44
Glasgu 41
Glendinning, Bishop Matthew 13, 25
glovers 15
Gododdin 22
golf 35
Goose Dubs 51
Gorbals 36, 41, 73
Gorbells 58
Gordon, Parson of Rothiemay 58
Gothic 13, 60, 65
Govan 24, 28, 40, 41-43, 49, 53
grammar school 14, 52, 60, 78
Grammar School Wynd 60
Grange 23
Grangehill 23
grassmarket 16
Gratian 79
Gregory, Susanna 78
Gregory IX 27
Greyfriars 44, 51, 60
Greyfriars' Port 51
Greyfriars' Wynd 52
Guild members 15
Guvan 41
Guven 41
Gyrth Burn 51

H

Haddington 49
Hadrian's Wall 22
Hael, Rhydderch 23
Halfpenny land of Car(r)ick 41
Hamilton 42, 43
hammermen 15
Heidelberg 82
Henry I 22
Henryson, Robert 36
Herbert, Bishop 10, 23, 24, 26, 41, 42, 43
Heriot, Alexander 36
Heselrig, William 32
Hesse, Herman 78
High Church 10
High Court of Justiciary 32
High Street 16, 18, 26, 44, 45, 50-54, 60, 61, 71, 72, 78, 79
Hoddam 40, 49
Hogganfield Loch 63
Holy Land 45
Home, John 33
hospital 13, 15, 36
Hospitals 14
hospitals 26
houses of the friars 13
Hugo, Victor 78
Huntingdon, Earl of 41
Hutoune, Johne 32

I

Industrial Revolution 78
Inglis 14
Ingram, Archdeacon 24
Ingram, Bishop 24, 26
Ingram Street 13, 40, 60
Innocent III 24, 36
Innocent VIII 51
inquest (of David) 32, 40-41, 43
Ireland 22, 23, 82
Irish 26
Irvine 33
Isles, Western 22, 27

J

jail 72
James I 27, 43
James II 27, 28, 34, 44, 79
James III 27, 28
James IV 27, 42
James V 27
James VI 27
Jedburgh 26
Jesus 66
Jocelin, Bishop 10, 23, 24, 25, 26, 43, 49, 65
Jocelin of Furness 23
John, Bishop 24, 25, 26, 40, 41, 43, 65
John, St 66
John Knox Street 62

K

Kathconnen 34
Kenmore 42
Kennedy, James 34
Kenneth II 22
Kentigern, St *see also St Mungo* 10, 11, 13, 15, 19, 22-25, 28, 40, 49, 50, 52, 60, 65, 74
Kentigern: De Vita Sua 23
Ker, Mark 33
Kilpatrick 33, 34
Kilpatrick hills 33
Kilwinning 23
Kilwinning Abbey 23
Kinclaith 40
King's College 61
King's College chapel 66
kingdoms, British 22
Kirkgait 45
Kirkintilloch 44
Kirkland of Cambusnethan 41
Kirklee 41
Kirk Port 51
Knox, John 10

L

labourers 13
Lady Chapel 52, 65
Lanark 14, 32, 44, 50
Lanark, Sheriffdom of 32
Lanark, sheriff of 32
Latin 74, 79, 80
Lawrence 33
leather 16
Lennox 28
Lennox, earl(s) of 23, 27, 34
leper 36, 73
Lepers 45
lepers 26, 45, 52
Leprosy 73
leprosy 73
leprous 73
leukemia 73
Leysyng 32
Life of Kentigern 23, 25
Lilliesleif 41
Lindsay, Adam 32
Lindsay, Patrick 16
Lindsay, Sir David 36, 37
Lindsay's Port 15
linen 15
Little St Kentigern's Chapel 52, 60
Loch Lomond 11, 25
Lochwood 42, 62
locksmiths 15
London 32
Lothian 22, 25, 41
Lothian, earl of 33
Louvain 44
lower town 15
Low Green 51
Lucius III 43
Lunan 28
Lund, archbishop of 24
Lyons 24
Lyons, archbishop of 24

M

M8 63
Macbeth 22
Macfarlane, Leslie 34
Machutus, St 52
Maines of the Lang Coit 41
Maitland 35
Malcolm 22
Malcolm II 22
Malcolm IV 32, 40, 41
Malcolm III 40
maltsters 15

Malveisin, Bishop William 24, 25
Manau 22
manses 13
Margaret, St 40
Margaret of Denmark 27
market(s) 10, 11, 14-16, 18, 43, 49, 71, 72, 74, 79-81
market, fish 16
market, horse 16
market, meal 16
market cross 15, 16, 18, 53, 71
marketplace 15
Mary, Queen of Scots 18, 32, 41
Maryhill 42
Mary I 27
Mary of Guise 32
Mary of Pity, St 66
masons 13
Mauchline 23
Melrose 23, 26
Melrose Abbey 23
Mercat Cross 54
merchant guildry 15
merchants 15
metalworkers 15
Methven, John 28
metropolitan university 18
Michael, Bishop 16, 24
Michaelmas 35, 36
Michelson, John 36
Mid Dam 53
mill 41
Miller, James 63
millers 53
Molendinar Burn 13, 15, 16, 24, 36, 49-54, 62, 63, 71, 74, 78
Molyndoner 36
Monachkeneran 33, 34
Monkland 40, 42
Montrose, Duke of 62
Montrose's Lodging 62
Monty Python and the Holy Grail 78
Morebattle 40
Morland 24
Muirhead, Bishop Andrew 45, 62
Muirhead, Thomas 45
Mungo, St *see also* St Kentigern 10, 22, 40, 41, 49, 63, 65, 66
Muthill 35

Muthill croft 54
mylne 41

N
Nechtansmere 22
necropolis 51, 62, 78
Neilson, John 36
Newbattle 33, 42
Newbattle, abbot of 33
Newbattle, Lord 33
Newbattle Abbey 42
Nicholas, St 13, 15, 26, 52
Nicholas Street 51
Nicholas v 27, 28, 44, 50
Niddrie Forest 41
Nidisdaill 41
Ninian 10
Ninian, St 13, 26, 49
Nithsdale 41
Norham 24
Norman 40, 49, 51, 65
Norman-French 40
Northampton 24
Northumbrians 22
Norvele, Margaret 34
Nudry Foster 41
nunnery, Dominican 52

O
Observant Franciscans 13, 16, 26, 50
Oggo 32
Old Aberdeen 61
Old Kilpatrick 33
Old Wynd 15, 51
On The Consolations of Philosophy 79
Order of Preachers 44
Owen 22
Owen the Bald 22
Oxford 82

P
Padua 82
Paisley 33, 34
Paisley, Abbey (of) 33, 65
Paris 45, 66, 82
parish 10
Parliament, Scottish 16, 27
Partick 28, 41, 42
Partick Thistle 79

Paschal II 24
Pasche 35
Paston Letters 80
Pathelanerhc 41
Paul, St 44
Peebles 40, 44
Perth 14, 15, 16
Perthec 41
Peter, St 44
Peters, Ellis 78
pewterers 15
Pictish 22
Picts 22
Pilgrimage 19
pilgrims 15, 19
plague 19, 27, 45, 51, 73
Plantagenet 43
pneumonic 73
Poldrait Burn 49, 53
Polmadie 41
Pont, Timothy 11, 13, 15, 16
Port Glasgow 79
ports 15
Possil 42
Possilpark 41
Prague 78
prebend(s) 24, 25, 43
prebendaries 13, 61
precentor 25
Presbyterian 65
Protestant 13, 16
Provan 42, 45, 62
Provan, Lord of 42
Provan, Lordship of 42
Provand's Lordship 10, 13, 45, 52, 58, 62, 70, 78, 79
Provan Hall 42, 45, 62
provost(s) 42

R
Ramsay, Allane 32
Ramshorn 40, 54
Rannald's Wynd 60
Ranulf of Hadintun 49
Ratenraw 36
Ratounraw 45
Ravenna 78
Rede, Martin 34

Reformation 13, 15, 18, 19, 37, 51, 52, 54, 60, 62, 63, 78
Reformation, Protestant 10, 16, 23, 32
Reformation, second Protestant 16
Renaissance 78
Renfrew 14, 24, 27, 28, 43, 44, 53, 62
Renfrewshire 13, 23
Rere Cross 26
Rheged 22
Richard 33
Riddrie 42
river 11, 15
Robert 45
Robert I 27, 42
Robert II 27, 28
Robert III 58
Robertone, Sir Alexander 45
Robroyston 42
Roche, St 13, 19, 45, 51, 73
Roder 42
Rollack 45
Rollox 45
Rollox, St 45, 73
Romantics 78
Rome 10, 24, 28, 33, 65
Rottenrow 16, 36, 40, 45, 50, 51, 52, 54, 81
Rottenrow Port 51
Roxburgh 34
Royal Infirmary 51, 63
Rutherglen 14, 28, 34, 53

S
Saint Elmo's Fire 79
Salerno 81
Salisbury Cathedral 24, 25
Salomon 24
Saltmarket 19, 49, 71, 79, 80
sang school 52
Saracen's Head Inn 60
Scandinavians 22
Scone 78
Scotia 22
Scotland 10, 13-15, 18, 22, 24, 28, 32, 33, 35, 36, 40, 52, 65, 73
Scotland, chancellor of 34
Scotland, Northern 22
Scots 22, 32
Scots College 66

Scott, Sir Walter 32
Scottish 24, 44, 51, 61, 63, 65, 79
Scottish crown 22
Sens 24
Serf, St 52
Sheriff Court of Lanark at Glasgow 32
Shettleston 41, 42, 43
Shields 41
shoemakers 15, 50
Shuttle Street 44
Simon, Cuthbert 34
siward, earl of Northumbria 22
skinners 15, 50, 53
Slezer 59, 61, 62, 79
Slezer, John 11, 78
smallpox 73
smiths 15
Solway 11, 25
Solway Firth 41
Somerled 26
song school 14
son of Alan 28
son of Samuel of Renfrew 33
Sorbonne 82
South Port 51
Spain 27
spina bifida 73
Stablegreen Port 51, 52, 73
Stainmore 26
St Andrew 66
St Andrews 10, 15, 19, 24, 25, 33, 34, 58, 61, 65
St Enoch Square 10, 60
Stewart 28, 40
Stewarts 28
Stirling 22, 36
Stirling Castle 66
St James Road 51
St Kentigern's Chapel 52, 60
St Machar's Cathedral 65

St Mary of Loreto and St Anne 13, 16, 18, 26, 52, 60, 74
St Mary of Melrose 49
St Mungo's widow 33
St Mungo Museum 63
St Nicholas' Church 59
St Nicholas Hospital 45, 52, 62
St Ninian's leper hospital 45
Stobo 41, 45
Stockwell croft 54
Stockwell Street 78
Strathclyde 11, 22, 32
St Roche 15
St Thenew's chapel 52
St Thenew's Gate 16, 49, 52
St Albans, Bishop Walter de 24, 27
St Andrews 10, 18, 33
St Andrews, archbishop of 33
St Andrews, bishop of 24, 34
St Kentigern 70
St Ninian 52
St Roche 45, 52
sub-dean 25
Sub-dean Port 51
succentor 25
Symmerhill' 35
syphilis 73

T

tailors 15
tanners 15, 53
taxation 14
Teviotdale 26
Thenew, St *see* St Enoch
the rector of Kilpatrick 33
Thomas, St 50, 51, 52
Thurstan, archbishop of York 24
Tigrim, Nicholas 36
tolbooth 11, 18, 19, 35, 36, 53, 59, 71, 72
Tolbooth Steeple 59
town clerk 42

town council 42
Townhead 36, 51
Traquair 40
treasurer 25, 62
Tron 16, 18
tron 71, 72
Tron Church 16
Trongate 15, 16, 19, 35, 49, 51, 52, 53, 54, 60, 79, 81
Tron Kirk 16, 18
Tron steeple 60
Tron Theatre 16, 52
True Cross 25
tuberculosis 73
Tudor, Margaret 27
Turnbull, Bishop 34, 44, 61
Turnbull, Bishop William 28
Turnbull, Walter 34
Turnbull, William 34, 79
typhoid 19
typhus 73
Tyrconnel, Hugh O'Donnell of 27

U

Ulster 27
university 13, 15, 18, 34, 44, 50, 52, 54, 58, 60, 61, 78, 79, 82
Upper Clyde burghs 14
upper town 15

V

Valence, Aymer de 27
vegetables 16
vicars choral 25
Vico Fullorum 16
Victorian(s) 62, 66
Vikings 22
Virgin Mary 19, 52, 66

W

Walcargate 16

Walensibus 32
Walkergate 49, 51, 53, 71
Wallace, William 32
Walter 28
wapinschawing 35
wapinschaws 35
Wardlaw, Bishop Walter de 28
War of Independence 26, 65
wars, Anglo-Scottish 23
waulk 16
waulking 53
Waverley 32
weavers 15, 53
Weaver Street 51
Wellpark Brewery 78
wells 16, 18
Welsh 22, 32
Welsh Annals 23
Wester Commons 42
Western Isles 26
West Graham Street 35
Westminster Abbey 65, 66
West Port 15, 16, 51
Whithorn 22
Whitsunday 35
William I, the Lion 26, 28, 41, 43, 49, 58
William II 24
Wishart, Bishop 26
Wishart, Bishop Robert 26, 28, 43, 65
Wishart, John 42
Wood, Thomas 32
wool 16

Y

York 10, 24, 40, 41
York, archbishop of 24
Yorkhill 79
Yule 35

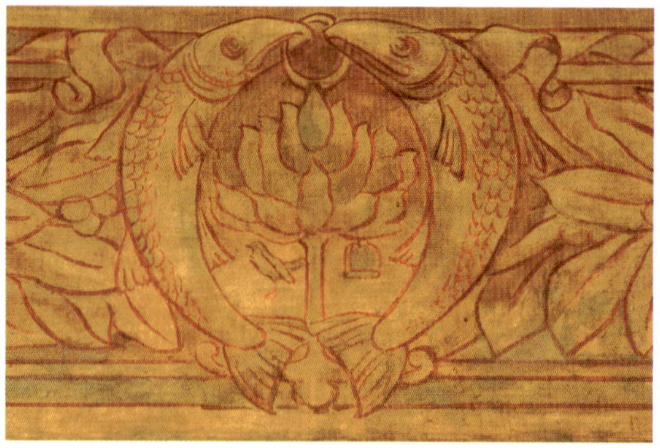